COUNTRY LIVING

THE PASSIONATE GARDENER

COUNTRY LIVING

THE PASSIONATE GARDENER

Edited by Miranda Innes

EBURY PRESS
LONDON

Published by Ebury Press
an imprint of Century Hutchinson Limited
20 Vauxhall Bridge Road
London SW1V 2SA

Editor: Gillian Haslam
Consultant Editor: Susan Conder
Designer: Tracey Lingwood

Filmset in Sabon by Advanced Filmsetters (Glasgow) Ltd
Printed and bound in Italy by New Interlitho S.p.a., Milan

British Library Cataloguing in Publication Data
Country living: the passionate gardener.
I. Great Britain. Gardens
I. Title
712'.6'0941

ISBN 0 85223 832 0

CONTENTS

INTRODUCTION

Gardening is a matter of inbuilt individuality, and there are as many different gardens as there are gardeners. Give two gardeners a packet of sweet pea seeds, and they will produce very different plants: the committed horticulturalist will trench, mulch and water and produce large, even-sized perfect specimens for cutting, trained up a utilitarian wigwam of canes or poles; and gardeners of a more tolerant cast will allow theirs to ramble, short-stemmed and unkempt, in wayward fashion along their rustic arbours.

There are those who favour the impeccable severity of gravel and clipped box, for whom nature is a force to be dominated, the garden as a blank canvas upon which to assert the superiority of man; and there are the romantic souls whose secateurs remain unused, and for whom nature can do no wrong. There are garden designers, whose efforts are directed towards making a tasteful, outdoor extension of the house, and there are plantsmen, whose borders flaunt a philistine disregard for harmony and layout. There are ecologists, whose gardens are a buzzing haven for butterflies, birds and insects, and there are the gardens of silent perfection, where vigilant battle against garden foes has inadvertently created a wildlife desert.

Gardening is a mercifully inexact science. Gardeners make their own discoveries and concoct their own secrets. Their labours are not usually fuelled by dogma or compulsion, and where rivalry exists, it rarely masks the underlying generosity which is the common denominator in horticultural circles. Gardeners are probably the kindest people in the world, overwhelmingly ready to share information, and to give away cuttings, seedlings and produce. The provenance of the plants in a passionate gardener's acreage will be a touching and fondly recalled autobiography. He or she may be vague about the precise names of the plants, but will be unlikely to forget whose gift they were in the first place. This is a common and endearing characteristic of the passionate gardener, whether humble or grand.

The gardens in this book represent a spectrum of style and purpose. The grand gardens tend to be older, distinguished by an enduring architectural structure. There is often an element of theatre in the plan and layout – the gardens of the rich and imaginative are, literally, scenery. They function as a manicured backdrop for the lives of their owners, sometimes many subsequent generations of one family. A different perspective of time means that there are mature trees, or saplings planted to give shade decades hence. The design is ambitious and encompasses the creation of lakes and mounds, topiary and *allees*, temples and follies. There are time and space enough to have a series of gardens – spring bulb corners, white and blue borders, whole areas devoted to the transitory charm of old-fashioned roses. Peacocks may strut, fountains may play, statues may gaze from a swirl of autumn leaves, and the mature trees of the deer park may border the garden.

But those of us who failed to be born the descendents of millionaires can burn with an equally strong passion for our smaller and equally demanding gardens. The archetypal example, at the modest end of the scale is the cottage garden: a mixture of the pretty and the practical, where no inch is wasted, flowers burgeon alongside vegetables and herbs, the clematis bower is just as charming for having a gnarled apple tree as host. Much of the cottage garden is ephemeral, this year's brilliant annuals will be gone by winter; the transitory beauty of hollyhocks, geraniums, wallflowers and dahlias, appear, disappear, and reappear elsewhere in the garden, unlike the grand garden where an enduring skeleton of stone and trees remains. Possibly this is why cottage gardeners are obsessives, and why their gardens are such friendly places to be, with a fine spirit of ingenuity about them. This is the fount of generosity – show a passing interest in the hebe or the cabbages, and you will leave with an embarrassment of cuttings and produce.

Finally, there are the gardens where horticultural passion has taken an oblique direction, where the garden has, intentionally or insidiously, begun to pay for itself. Fragrant borders have yielded dried flowers, pot pourri and a healthy business; flowers

have been forsaken for a sound economic fascination with vegetables; or the plants have become a mutable backdrop for an unusual open air sculpture gallery.

People who love gardens often do so with a quiet fanaticism. They can tell you where the fox passes at dawn, and will still be trimming and pruning when the snails are lured out by darkness. They will seriously grieve the loss of a frost-stricken ceanothus, and will invest their plants with positively anthropomorphic personality, confusing the visitor with casual references to "he" (a spreading mulberry tree) or "she" (a Great Maiden's Blush rose). Unlike most passions, this one is entirely benign. There are no serious crimes committed in its name (unless you call a spiky border of scarlet and orange dahlias criminal); people do not die for their gardens, nor kill for them. On the contrary, gardens seem to have visible life-enhancing and life-prolonging virtues. And gardeners, as a group, are the kindest and most peaceable of people. This is a most therapeutic passion.

Elisabeth Clutterbuck's bantams, decorative marauders in the herbaceous border

GRAND
GARDENS

VICTOR MONTAGU

Victor Montagu, whose ancestors were showered with titles by Charles II, and one of whom invented the sandwich, has spent more than 30 years making his mark on Mapperton

The beautiful, secluded and romantic Italian gardens at Mapperton lie in a deep valley in lush farmland near Beaminster in West Dorset. They are approached through the courtyard of a splendid Jacobean house, with balconied, gabled roofs and barley-twisted chimneys. Beyond the house is a wide lawn, and from the edge of this smooth expanse, the Italian gardens are visible in a deep valley. Within the gardens are an orangery, rose pergolas, topiary, statuary and flower beds; massive retaining walls, a stone stair-case from the lawn to the terraces and a 17th-century garden house overlooking two oblong carp pools, stocked with golden orfe.

The Italian gardens fill the entire valley, des-cending through a wild, woodland garden to a pastoral landscape where a little stream runs south to join the River Brit at Bridport, the model for Thomas Hardy's 'Port Bredy'.

This is one of the few post-Edwardian gardens to remain largely in its original condition. It was laid out between 1919 and 1927 by Mrs Labouchère on the basis of an ancient terraced garden, and has been owned and improved since 1955 by the Hon Victor Edward Paulet Montagu.

An aqueous mirror reflecting the sky, and flanked by topiary

Montagu bought the house because of his political connection with Dorset, and because it was close to land owned by his Paulet ancestors. In 1962 he succeeded as the 10th Earl of Sandwich, Baron Montagu of St Neots, and Viscount Hinchingbrooke, but he disclaimed the titles for life in 1964 in order to continue with his career in the House of Commons.

Montagu created the wild, woodland garden leading to the fields and woods beyond the Italian Garden. He planted limes to replace the dying elms, laid out the new flower beds, removed a thicket of dense yew trees which had blocked off the vista to the south of the garden, reinforced the massive retaining walls, and planted hundreds of flowering shrubs. It was not all plain sailing, though, as his garden diary of the time shows, with such gems as: "Peacocks ate plants. Plants died."

He also moved a rose pergola from the north end of the valley to the middle of the Italian garden, and built a substantial orangery in its place. Apart from that, his policy has been to conserve what was originally there, to improve on this where necessary, and to keep the gardens open to the public.

Victor Montagu has retired from public life and the management of the gardens has been delegated to John and Caroline Montagu, his eldest son and daughter-in-law.

John and Caroline have children and each has a separate professional life in London, but they come to Dorset almost every weekend to work and plan for the estate's future. They are also committed to Victor Montagu's tradition of public access.

The Montagus are one of England's oldest and most interesting families. Sir Edward Montagu, the "My Lord" of Samuel Pepys's *Diary*, fought in the Civil War for Oliver Cromwell, but he and Pepys were also instrumental in the restoration of the monarchy, for which the grateful Charles II rewarded Sir Edward with three titles and other benefits in 1660. John, the 4th Earl, sponsored Captain James Cook in his discovery of the Sandwich (Hawaiian) Islands and was the originator of the first sandwich, a slice of rare beef between two slices of bread which he could eat without having to leave the gaming table.

Mrs Labouchère employed a large team of gardeners, which had been reduced to four by the time that Victor Montagu took possession, but the garden can now afford only two part-time gardeners. The elder of these is William Kennedy, a friendly, hard-working, enthusiastic man. "Mapperton is sheer magic," he confides. "It's a holiday for me to be working here." The gardens are listed Grade II, but since they contain no listed monuments they do not qualify for any statutory grant. The upkeep is considerable, and the moulded statuary is crumbling as a result of over 60 years' exposure to frost and sun.

John and Caroline Montagu and their children are slightly apprehensive of the work in front of them as they strive almost unaided to preserve Mapperton, but it is likely that the family which was able to restore the monarchy, find Hawaii and invent the sandwich will also be able to restore these beautifully designed and situated gardens. "The trend at Mapperton has to be upwards," John Montagu explained. In recent years there has been a Summer Fair in the courtyard, usually in August, with craft stalls, teas and children's events, in aid of local churches and a national charity, and occasional summer outdoor events, such as a Summer Spectacular with fireworks, have been held.

According to Pevsner, part of the great charm of Mapperton is the vagueness between what is private and what is public. The gardens are under-visited and secluded; pilgrims often find they are alone, even in the height of summer, and feel more like a house guest than a paying customer. Even the family motto, *Post tot naufragia portum* ("After so many shipwrecks, a port!"), reflects the garden's tranquillity.

*Above John and Caroline Montagu, with their daughter Jemima and family dog,
at the top of the walled garden*
Right Italianate elements of statuary and topiary, enlivened by a passing duck
*Overleaf The architecture of Mapperton provides a glorious framework for more ephemeral
herbaceous planting*

ELISABETH CLUTTERBUCK

*In a secret garden showing the hand of Capability Brown,
Elisabeth Clutterbuck is a protective guardian
to a legacy of family and horticultural history*

A matter of miles from Oxford's "base and brickish" industrial zone lies a garden of peaceful green trees and soothing fragrances. Turning into the courtyard of Wootton Place is like stepping back a century or so; beyond the impenetrable yew hedges is a world of cooing doves and soughing trees, where the sound of transparently fine china clinking under the walnut tree, and of croquet mallet striking against ball, would not be out of place.

Elisabeth Clutterbuck, who lives here, disputes the weighty feeling of tradition that permeates house and garden: "Oh, we haven't been here very long, not even 100 years." Here time moves slowly, and allows for careful and leisurely changes. There is time and space to let the ancient holm-oak regenerate after the bitter frost of 1983, and to let the massive lightning-riven wellingtonia recover from its injuries. The weathered components of this garden, the giant trees that are its bones, are treated with reverence. Mrs Clutterbuck's father, Canon Marriott, used to take off for Norway whenever one of them had to be felled, waiting anxiously in exile for word from his gardener, Alfred Gubbins, that all traces of the departed tree had been tactfully obliterated.

He also threatened to return and haunt his daughter should anything be allowed to damage the perfect lawns.

An ilex – "we always called it the swing tree" – and a huge walnut, with branches as big as the trunks of most other trees, have stood sentinel over the house for almost 500 years, and the rest of the garden was constructed around them. It took its present shape in about 1740. Canon Marriott was justly proud of it, and saw in the design the hand of a master. A clue to his identity came from one Barrington Buggins, who was a carpenter at the house when Elisabeth was a girl. He told her father that his grandfather knew the man who laid out the garden, and that he used to come over after a day's work at Blenheim.

Confirmation of the identity of this great garden designer did not come until much later. Some years ago Mrs Clutterbuck was in the garden: "I was on my knees weeding as usual. I was suddenly conscious that someone was standing behind me. A woman was there, wearing a flat hat with a scarf round it, carrying a huge knapsack. I had no idea who she was. We walked round the garden in perfect silence, and then she suddenly said 'Yes, oh yes! I see the master's

Left   *Geometric flower beds engulfed in colour, in full view of a magnificent wooden seat*
Above   *Elisabeth Clutterbuck with* Veratrum *'Jasper', named after her son*

hand.' In complete ignorance I asked 'Who do you mean by the master?' 'Why, Brown of course.' I still had no idea who she meant."

The woman turned out to be Dorothy Stroud, the eminent authority on Capability Brown. The garden bears many of his hallmarks, with its clumps of handsome evergreens. And it has a lovely secret garden whose 14-feet-high walls are decked with characteristic stone spheres. Not long ago, a large stretch of this honey-coloured wall collapsed. Specialists came from far away, and gloomily gave enormous estimates of the cost to repair it. Arthur Lewington, Mrs Clutterbuck's gardener and occasional knight in shining armour, rebuilt it himself. "I just popped it back up," he says casually.

The wall is part of the eclectic history of the place. Everything has a pedigree, though nothing is predictable. A handsome stone seat embowered by jasmine and clematis came from Chequers, which used to be the Clutterbuck home. Rampant violas came from a Scottish croft, clumps of white crinum from a local cottage garden, and a unique yellow *Veratrum* 'Jasper', named after Mrs Clutterbuck's son, is a hybrid from the wild plant that she brought back from an Alpine expedition.

For a little while, the family name was immortalised by *Primula Clutterbuckii*. Hugh, Elisabeth's husband, was an explorer. "Not a specialist," she says with characteristic modesty, "just an intelligent sort of chap." On a trip to the Himalayas with Kingdon Ward, he discovered a yellow primula which looked like a tiny daffodil. Seeds were brought back to England and placed with five of the most reputable botanical gardens in Britain. Alone, the Edinburgh specimen flourished, and Hugh Clutterbuck flew up to see it in flower. It was christened, and promptly disappeared, never to be seen again.

As well as echoes of times past, the garden is outstanding for the range of plants in its four acres. Each spring, the ground beneath the cherry trees glows with daffodils – over 100 different varieties, dating from 1900, many of which have now disappeared elsewhere. They multiplied through a charming family tradition started by Elisabeth's mother. Every winter from 1900 onwards, the house would be filled with containers of new kinds of forced daffodils which were planted out after flowering. Over the decades they have spread and been added to – a friend of Mrs Clutterbuck's hybridises new pink and white varieties – to achieve their sumptuous present-day cloth-of-gold effect.

Swathes of colour from delphiniums, geraniums, achillea and shrubby potentillas, in massed banks against rose-covered outbuildings

Of the roses, Arthur says with affection, "There are hundreds of them," many of which date back to Capability Brown's time. Some are so old that Graham Thomas, a friend and frequent visitor to the garden, hesitated to name them. But Mrs Clutterbuck is not a rose purist: "They don't all have to be 1750. I like them all mixed up with lovely modern ones – 'Mermaid' of course, and 'Constance Spry'. I'm very fond of 'Fantin Latour', and 'Empress Josephine' which is like a big peony, pink with mauvy petals dotted about." And there is a 'Kiftsgate' which envelops a tall holly tree with its breathtaking white flowers each summer. This is a notoriously aggressive rose. Arthur advised: "For God's sake don't put it on your house, it grows 14 to 16 feet a year. I know someone who did, and now they can't do a

thing with it." In his opinion, the trees make the garden, and there is a fine profusion of them. There were many different cedars and pines originally, including a Himalayan deodar, of which Arthur is especially fond.

The remark that perfectly captures the particular charm of this garden was made back in balmy Edwardian days by a friend of Mrs Clutterbuck. Andrew Shirley, aged six, and Elisabeth, aged five, were walking round the garden with her mother, who said to the solemn little boy: "You really like this garden, don't you Andrew?" To which he replied "Yes I do. It's so secret. The essence of a garden is surprise."

He was right. Wootton Place is a garden of hidden corners and unexpected glimpses of breathtaking beauty, such as the laburnum arch at the end of a green walk, or the sheet of glossy golden aconites which shine up at the grey February sky. There are scented pockets of osmanthus, sarcococca and daphnes; and the sun-warmed drowsiness of old-fashioned roses. When the Georgian windows to the veranda are removed each spring, they reveal a rich tapestry of bloom. A 'Mary Wallace' rose scrambles up to the bedroom windows over less vigorous climbers – passionflower, *Cobaea scandens*, morning glory, old-fashioned perennial sweet peas, climbing geraniums and a venerable lemon verbena which has repaid its protective nurturing by scenting the air for one and a half centuries.

The pleasure and the pain of gardening are symbolized by Mr Lewington's sweet peas: 100 of them, lovingly grown and potted on over the winter, the best in the country, found dead as a doornail after a particularly vicious frost. Sorrowfully he tipped them out of their pots. "They're gone. Shocking job isn't it. Tends to put you off gardening." Then, seeing his ancient 'Harpur Crewe' wallflowers which had made it through the winter, he said "You don't do it for money, you just do it for the love of it."

JOHN FOWLER

*In his peaceful Hampshire garden
John Fowler used his decorator's eye
to combine an adventurous taste in
colour with a formal design*

Neat white Versailles tubs and Chippendale-inspired garden seats are all the rage for the well dressed garden. Their use, along with trellis arbours and stone vases, has been inspired by history, but also, certainly, by the influence of the famous interior decorator, John Fowler.

John Fowler was born in 1906 into a world very different from that of the great houses he later came to inhabit. He had no formal education in art and design, but taught himself in afternoons spent wandering round London's Victoria & Albert Museum. He designed wallpapers, then furniture, and in the 1930s he was one of the group of artists working in the decorative furniture studio of Peter Jones. He set up in business with a group of friends in 1935, farther down London King's Road.

Three years later his talents were spotted by society hostess Sibyl Colefax, a lady of zeal and considerable talent who loved to decorate the houses of her friends. They formed the firm Colefax & Fowler, which has become part of the decorating history of our century, famous for its delicious fabrics and wallpapers, and the absolute arbiter of taste in the restoration of 18th-century interiors.

John Fowler found the rambling Georgian house at 39 Brook Street in Mayfair, which is still the firm's headquarters, just before the end of the war. He still lived in the King's Road, but when

Left *Whimsical Dutch gables and crisply pointed
gate-posts, set off by expanses of perfectly
manicured lawn*
Overleaf *A stone shepherd guards the passage between
two tall hedges of immaculately clipped hornbeam*

the war ended he looked round for a country retreat, and he bought the Hunting Lodge at Odiham in Hampshire, which is now owned by The National Trust. What amused and attracted him about the lodge was its fanciful Gothick façade, added in the 18th century purely for decoration so that it could play its part as an eye-catcher in the designed landscape around Dogmersfield Park. The façade had been built on to a minute keeper's cottage, which had grown a little over the years and which John Fowler enlarged further, but it always retained its doll's house character.

Though John Fowler could not help but give good, informal advice on the gardens of his friends, the Hunting Lodge is the only garden known to have been designed by him. His friends say it has changed somewhat in character since his death in 1977, but it is beautifully conserved in both structure and health, and it still illustrates its maker's tastes.

In 1946 the lodge sat in a woodland clearing overlooking a small lake. This clearing is as impeccably organised and proportioned as a French château's parterre or an English Palladian mansion. The 'frame' of the garden is the wide gravel path enclosing a rectangle of green. The relationship between this rectangle and the square paved area occupied by the lodge and its terrace exactly mirrors the classical relationship of hall to salon in the Palladian interiors of Holkham and Kedleston Halls, both places John Fowler knew well. In the garden this was almost certainly achieved by his instinctive feel for the right proportions, rather than by painstaking measurement.

At the time John Fowler was laying out his garden, he was also changing partners; Lady Colefax's interest in the firm was being taken over by Mrs Nancy Lancaster. It was at her former home, Ditchley Park in Oxfordshire, that John Fowler had seen Geoffrey Jellicoe's curving wall of water that closed the formal parterre

Right   *A weathered stone ornament surrounded by roses and honeysuckle*
Overleaf   *The neat Gothick pavilion, hidden by a green veil of hops and flanked by pots of agapanthus. The clipped box crisply punctuates the expanse of green*

garden vista, inspired by the famous garden room at Villa Gamberaia in Tuscany. John Fowler's green-clipped country version was the perfect adaptation of this sophisticated idea. If the lodge façade holds as dominant a position in the garden as the fireplace in a room, then the topiary hedges of clipped hornbeam are as balanced as the formal positions for sofas. The fashion for hedges on stilts had been demonstrated in England in the 30s at Hidcote Manor and Sissinghurst Castle gardens; here they add lightness and freedom. They allow intriguing glimpses of other parts of the garden, in much the same way as the pillars of a classical screen.

The Gothick pavilions are both reflections of the lodge's façade, and more solid recreations of many 'Vogue Regency' curtain designs that John Fowler liked to use in country houses. The taste for Regency design had revived in the 20s when he was learning his trade; its lightness and sense of fun appealed to him.

The original pieces of garden furniture – delicate metal seats painted white, and white Gothick armchairs – were all inspired by Regency designs, and John Fowler placed them around the garden as carefully as if he were placing gilded and brocaded chairs within a room. On the brick terrace he balanced seats each side of the garden door, and ranged the white Versailles tubs, filled with pink and scarlet geraniums, as a terrace edging. In the garden the chairs and small tables are in conversational gatherings, with pairs of vases flanking 'doorways' and painted wooden obelisks set as eye-catchers in the outer garden and wood. A painted wooden Pekinese dog sat beside the garden door.

In planting his garden, John Fowler's taste was also impeccable, though his knowledge of plants was probably confined to those he liked. In the descriptions of his choices given by his cousin, the garden designer Barbara Oakley, there is similarity between his taste and that of Vita Sackville-West. He had her love of old roses, especially the scented hybrid musks reared by the Rev. Pemberton – 'Felicia', 'Cornelia' and 'Penelope'. At the Hunting Lodge, as at Sissinghurst, 'Madame Alfred Carrière' clambered over the brickwork and 'Adelaide

d'Orléans' scrambled into the trees. He, too, used the red stems of dogwood to cheer his visitors' arrivals in winter, and his orchard primavera of wild daffodils, fritillaries and anemones to charm them in spring.

Sibyl Colefax was a great friend of the Nicolsons and a frequent visitor to Sissinghurst. John Fowler must have enjoyed its garden (which he would have seen in its first flowering immediately before the war) and the way Harold Nicolson had transformed its initial awkwardness into wonderfully pleasing vistas and symmetrical enclosures. John Fowler achieved this at the Hunting Lodge as well, but in a much less complicated way. He would also have enjoyed Sissinghurst's luxuriance of flowers, planted by Vita Sackville-West as the natural corollary to formality of design, in the same way as the frills and flounces of exquisite chintzes adorned a Georgian window.

But John Fowler's use of colours in interior design was far more adventurous than Vita's colour sense in her garden, and even farther removed from the steadfast rules laid down by Gertrude Jekyll. He would mix warm and cool colours together with great verve; apricot terracotta walls with vivid blue Delft china, chintzes of roses in reds and pinks with bluey-green leaves, and cream ivory satins trimmed with bright turquoise ribbon. He loved to use white, and had 'Iceberg' roses in his garden but, to him, white was not a simple colour. In his decoration of the hall at Syon House, he used a subtle mix of blue/white, palest lavender blue, soft white and almost cream. Though he has left no record of particular colour combinations for flowers, it would be fascinating to experiment, using as examples the rooms he painted at Clandon or Syon or Sudbury: the unusual partnership of colours, such as yellow-greens with creams, golds and browns; or warm red with white, grey and electric blue.

These might be unconventional or unusual garden schemes, but they might well prove that the sure eye of a master is good for all seasons. When the outdoor room is treated with the same degree of detailed care and attention as the decoration of an indoor room, the creative art of gardening assumes endless possibilities.

ELIZABETH MACLEOD MATTHEWS

*At Chenies Manor, fondly haunted by Henry VIII,
Elizabeth Macleod Matthews has created an
exquisite garden of the senses*

Elizabeth MacLeod Matthews is a small, dark, vital woman with three shadows: her dogs Caspar, Cecil and Sholto. She exudes enthusiasm as she talks about the garden she loves. It is at Chenies Manor, near Rickmansworth, the oldest inhabited brick-built house in England. She and her husband Alastair bought it in 1956. Henry VIII stayed there – indeed he haunts it – and he copied its carved brick chimneys at Hampton Court. While the four-acre Tudor Great Garden at Chenies Manor has been lost, partly under farm buildings, the old Little Gardens have been restored to nearly their original shape, yet they bear the strong stamp of Elizabeth's gardening taste.

A country child, she had been given a tiny garden under a bush – "Children always get a garden in the worst position" – and her first gardening memories are of marigolds. But, unlike the majority of children, "I rapidly asked for something better, and by the time I was six I had quite a nice little bed. When I was 12 years old I was given a larger patch, two beds with a bit of rock garden and a path with a wrought-iron gate at the end. I was keen on rock plants then and was very proud of my *Anemone pulsatilla*. Later I took over an empty greenhouse and started growing carnations. I was about 14. I had pots and pots of them. It was so satisfying; they grew so easily."

"Then I discovered a very old book on sweet peas which told you exactly what to do; the trench had to be six feet deep. I dug most of it, right down into the subsoil, perhaps not quite that deep but when I was in it I couldn't see over the top. My father's gardener helped a bit, and my parents got quite worried as we went trenching away across the kitchen garden. I followed the instructions most diligently, starting with newspaper at the bottom and then farmhouse manure mixed with soil – by hand if it was all lumpy. It's logical, because as the roots go down you must feed them evenly or the lengths of stem between the blooms are uneven, frightfully important for exhibiting. I won some prizes when I was about 16, still following this marvellous old book, and I used to bring bucketloads in to give to my mother.

"Since then I have never *not* grown sweet peas. Robert Bolton's seed is best, I always sow it on 25 September. I grow various colours for different rooms; mauvey black ones are so striking with blue flowers in the drawing room, and I love the long-stemmed white ones for the dining room on hot evenings. There is just one week when the old-fashioned roses are perfect; I have a party and do an arrangement of roses and sweet peas."

She took out all the Hybrid Tea roses – "clashy colours and straggly stems with a beautiful blodge on top" – and planted 'The Fairy', a late-season, sugar-pink polyanthus with tiny double flowers.

*Elizabeth, surrounded by box, bergenias, stachys, cotoneaster
and a pair of family spaniels*

"It's adorable, so pretty with the alchemilla and white nicotiana, and it lasts so well in water.

"I have never been without a garden. When I first met Alastair he had a country cottage near my parents with a pretty little garden that had become rather derelict: it had old roses and typical herbaceous stuff in a nice cottagey mixture. He went away for a while, so I put my tools in the car and gave it a clean up, much to his surprise. I wasn't in love, I was sorry for the garden."

But love must have crept in because they married and lived for a year commuting between the cottage and Alastair's London flat. Then Chenies Manor came on the market. "Alastair has always loved old houses. It had been divided up and had had refugees in it, but he saw the potential – and I fell in love with the garden, or rather what I could make of it."

Chenies, which has been a farmhouse since about 1620, had previously belonged to the Bedfords, but they moved to Woburn and it was let cheaply to farming tenants because it was so old and cumbersome. "When we came here, there were chicken-runs and a big cedar in the front courtyards, but the water table fell – London had drunk it all up – and the tree died." Behind the house was a weeping ash, which may be the largest in Europe, and a Wellingtonia, "dark and near the house, but I should loathe to have it out as it acts as a lightning conductor". Apart from

these, there were only some Victorian paths and a great many laurel hedges with mandrakes growing underneath. "They have forked roots, like a man's legs, and are quite difficult to get out. I still have some in the Physic Garden."

Elizabeth started, with typical energy, on the site of the Little Gardens, west of the house. "The first thing I did was to build a low wall right across from north to south." Behind it was a depression which tallied with a small garden marked on an early plan, so they based their design on the sunken Tudor Pond Garden at Hampton Court. "Alastair dug it out with a tractor, and my father gave me a birthday present of two builders who levelled the terraces and put in the stonework."

Two years after they bought the house, Alastair's business took him to New York. "We lived there for a year and I soaked myself in garden history. When I came back I knew what I wanted and sliced through ours with the yew avenue." This is like the yew walk at Sissinghurst. It runs at right angles to the wall Elizabeth built and cuts the garden into quarters, giving it a dark, mysterious backbone, with the sunken garden to the north and the White Garden to the south.

The old York stone and firm topiary give the sunken garden visual strength, while perennials with good foliage, such as tall flag irises in the central fountain, bergenias, hostas, Solomon's

The sunken garden at Chenies in early summer, with a perfectly balanced colour scheme of
cool blue and acid yellow, studded with scarlet

seal and astrantia, make a base for the more colourful plants which are set out in blocks. Spring flowers and apple blossom are followed by an early-summer scheme of clean mauve-blue and white with the lime yellow of *Alchemilla mollis*. It is light and fresh, with catmint exactly matching the blue of tall *Campanula latiloba*, some of which is white; purple *C. glomerata*; mauve hosta flowers, creamy spires of *Sisyrinchium striatum* and silver *Stachys lanata*. By August the blues have gone and the sunken garden is all warm golds, oranges and reds. African marigolds and rudbeckias are ablaze, but they are cooled and softened by the silvers. "I used to hate oranges and yellows, but as long as you keep to soft pinks and blues early on you can enjoy hot colours in late summer – and the visitors love them. I still can't find the right blue for the weeks between the campanulas and the asters."

The White Garden was planned as a topiary garden: "I found the four large birds and a small bird and a bush like a column with a ball on top for the middle, but it died from growing over a secret underground passage; plants don't like to be on top of them. Luckily I was given a statue of a little boy, so he went in the middle instead." The secret passages date back to an earlier 13th-century house and form an extensive system, possibly used as an escape route during the Wars of the Roses and probably useful in the Civil War too.

Elizabeth grew all the box edgings herself from cuttings, "just putting them in a little trench of sand". At first the topiary garden was planted with herbs, but these proved so interesting that she took in a field at the back, which later became the Physic Garden, and moved them there. They were replaced with white flowers, and the topiary garden became the White Garden, her favourite place. "Sometimes we eat supper out there – it's all very romantic. White gardens are for the night; and the scent of the tobacco plant is unbelievable. Sometimes on hot nights I water the garden at two o'clock in the morning. You can't imagine how peaceful it is." It contains subtle shades of white lilies, roses, pinks, delphiniums, campanulas, violas, geraniums, foxgloves, tulips in spring and agapanthus and phlox in late summer.

The Physic Garden, like the turf maze, copied from a Tudor portrait at Woburn which also shows the garden at Chenies, is perfectly in keeping with the house. The Physic Garden has a serious purpose too, planned with the help of Dr Denis Tweddle, who worked for the Wellcome Foundation, and includes medicinal plants, as well as some for dyeing and scent, and culinary herbs. It is laid out round an old octagonal well-house – always locked because the well itself is 180 feet deep – with a pointed roof and white walls on which is trained the sweet-scented rose 'Paul's Lemon Pillar'. When the herbs are in flower it is the prettiest place in the garden.

To walk round with Elizabeth is to appreciate her great love of plants, her experience and skill – not always conventional. "A vine came as a cutting from Milton's cottage at Chalfont St Giles, but it took a long time to get going until I started giving it all the visitors' tea-bags, and now it's fine." She makes grape jelly from this vine, using an old American recipe. Nearby is a gabled ruin. "When we came here it was covered with ivy and was just a green mound. I wanted something romantic, spring-like, so I planted the big scented musk rambler 'Bobbie James'. The flowers are so like blossom and it covers the old brickwork without hiding it. There should be something growing on the corner, but – it's so tedious – secret passages run underneath and things start well and then fade away.

"I don't like tired plants, so I strip off all the damaged leaves and there is a completely fresh plant. We had a snail explosion two years ago – I think people used to eat them around here – and they were making holes in all the hosta leaves. I used to go out every night with a torch and collect hundreds of them. It was horrific. There's nothing so telling as eaten hosta leaves, it's such slack gardening. Now I buy slug killer by the sack." In the kitchen garden, once full of vegetables, now grow rows of flowers for the house and for sale: "In the 1960s we cleared it of several tons of rubble. I used to dig it and made myself take out five stones with every forkful – it gave it a rhythm." To convey an idea of the scale, she plants 300 gladioli every year. There is now a "flower factory" in a new barn over the crypt-cum-dungeon. Downstairs is an exhibition of garden history, one of her great interests, and nearby an excellent shop and plant stall.

Asked about her favourite plants, she says they are all about equal "like the pieces in a patchwork quilt. What matters is that they should fit in together – except for sweet peas of course – and I do love foxgloves. I feel terribly guilty if I have to pull one up, and I always try to find it a new home. They give height, and the white ones are so lovely at night."

She knows she can never stop gardening or thinking about gardening. Future plans include a new kitchen garden layout, autumn-flowering crocuses, and more roses.

THE EARL OF DONOUGHMORE

A billow of roses, peacocks on the grass, and the sound of bells – the Earl of Donoughmore's Bampton Manor has it all

Bampton Manor has the sort of garden reminiscent of summer afternoons and tinkling teacups, of long-limbed, perfect youth racing down the gravel to the tennis court – "Wimbledon players would find our game a little hard to recognise", says the Earl of Donoughmore – church bells, and drowsy heat-lulled conversations floating from the rose bower.

It was designed originally in the 1940s by Countess Munster, whose equally gifted sister designed the garden at Pusey. Bampton Manor is the miniaturised version. Both have a controlled profusion of herbaceous borders, handsome trees,

artfully natural-looking water and great walled vegetable gardens, but Pusey is set in an 18th-century landscape, with views of undulating hills, while Bampton is on the outskirts of a village, and walled, hedged and enclosed, where every view is of the works of man.

Some of the more recent changes in the garden were instigated by the urgent need for subjects to paint – Lady Donoughmore and one of their four sons, Nicholas Hely Hutchinson, are both painters. She creates delicate and minutely observed floral still lives, and Nicholas has a more exuberant touch with landscapes and the garden,

Above   *The Earl with his wife and son, Nicholas, both of whom are painters deriving inspiration from the garden*
Right   *A lichen-covered urn in a setting of rugosa roses*
Overleaf   *The celebrated double border, backed by a contrasting row of Irish yew and with a pale cloud of* Crambe cordifolia *overspilling the wide lawn path*

in the simple, colourful and powerful style of Matisse or Dufy.

As a result, the vegetable garden has surprising eruptions of sunflowers, dahlias and delphiniums, among the orderly rows of asparagus, fruit trees and standard gooseberries. The latter are much approved of by the Earl: "Jolly good things – you don't have to bend down to pick them."

The family also did away with the iris bed in front of the house, and replaced it with a lavender hedge. Irises, however glorious in their prime, flower only briefly, and for the rest of the year look no more glamorous than a motley and tattered collection of broken umbrellas. And as Lady Donoughmore says: "They're so difficult to cope with. They're very moody things." The biggest and most daunting task was tackling the great corridor of herbaceous borders, which had ebulliently overflowed, so the two sides met in the middle. Everything had to be moved back: "It was an enormous job – very difficult to put the right plants in the right places because you do it when they're all dormant, so you can't really see what they are."

The soil, which is basically chalk, supports a great wealth of bloom. There are festoons of roses: " 'Madame Grégoire Staechelin'– such a stunning rose, but she only does it once", 'New Dawn', 'Golden Showers' and *Rosa moyesii* 'Geranium' with enormous orange autumn rosehips. Like all gardeners who have weakened at the onslaught of catalogue hype, Lady Donoughmore has created a handful of garden mismatches: a peevish bicker between mauve tulips and their peachy neighbours, and the puce rose 'William Lobb', next to a golden rose. "If they're the wrong colour, they always flourish like mad."

But of all the arguments in the garden, none is as shrill as the sound of their pet peacocks. They are far more stupid than chickens; they flaunt themselves at the local fox population; they commit casual genocide. "The father kills his offspring because he reckons that they're taking the food that he's about to want to eat – he stamps on them." They eschew plants, but they do make dust-baths wherever possible. Preening in front of their personal mirror, wolfing down currants for tea (augmented by turkey pellets and brown bread) and shrieking like an express train are their favourite pastimes. If you are looking for peace, it's best to give peacocks a miss.

An avenue of pollarded limes in front
of the manor house

LORD AND LADY BATH

*Lord and Lady Bath's private Wiltshire garden is
a sentimental scrapbook of 30 years' companion planting,
begun with the gift of a mulberry tree*

Lord and Lady Bath live in an old silk-mill, a place of enchantment surrounded by sloping gardens which they have created together over the years.

When they moved in, there was only a phalanx of black poplars, dour guardians of the mill, with the waters of the Wylye cavorting under the house and the ruin of a tiny cottage – just floor and fireplace – cupped in the hillside. Now, a generation later, the river still laps at the back door, but time and affectionate alteration have made it a different place. The valley is now terraced, like green paddy-fields stretching up the hillside. The broad stillness of the Wylye has a little nesting island for ducks, and reflects a gothic tracery of great arching, lichenous trees above a fringe of pollarded red willows. The sparkling weir behind the eelhouse reflects a fractured kaleidoscope of tulips, candelabra primulas, an *Acer pseudoplatanus* 'Brilliantissimum' – "which may be a mistake there, but may be just all right" – as well as the demure charm of a naiad statue beneath a weeping pear tree.

The ruined cottage now has a surreal air, furnished with foxglove spires, self-sown wallflowers and wild strawberries. Above, the valley is sculpted with ramparts of yew, a green fortress concealing a maze of outdoor rooms, doored and windowed, beyond which are fragrant roses.

Past a generous herbaceous border, with great areas of pure colour from Oriental poppies, up stone steps, past a pair of whimsical topiary birds flanking a curlicued gate – "I do those – they're meant to be wrens, nice little fat ones" – is the wild garden, Lady Bath's joy and tribulation. "I love this corner – I am allowed wild things here, even daisies, which I love."

Lord and Lady Bath do not see eye to eye about everything horticultural. She has a love of unruly plants, weeds even, that he just cannot abide: "Indeed he weedkills them." Now they have evolved a comfortable congruence of differing garden styles. An errant goat prematurely pollarding the willows, or a froth of cow parsley, where none should be, produces nothing worse than a wrinkle in the lordly brow. Here, in spite of a sward of apparently vigorous seedling lilies, Lady Bath bemoans their fragility: "I've always failed with lilies – they just fade away. But the successes make you so happy that you forget the failures."

Failures are not apparent. There is a medieval carpet of fritillaries, trilliums, erythroniums (their favourite flower), white bluebells ("I love them so much, but they do rather take over the more unusual things"), *Viola labradorica* ("Vita Sackville-West sent me that. She was so kind – I just wrote to her to ask where I could get hold of some, and she sent me some little roots") and cowslips, beneath a multicoloured canopy of viburnum, pieris, azaleas and camellias.

Despite his aversion to untamed nature, Lord and Lady Bath have a regular romantic tryst in

Lord and Lady Bath, dressed for gardening, under their mulberry tree, with Rutty and Maria

this spot: "Sunset is wonderful – we always come up here to get the last of the sun."

In passing, the evening sun gilds a large mulberry tree that grows by the rose garden, a symbol of the mutual affection of the creators of this much-loved garden. "We brought the mulberry from our former house. It was about 15 years old, already large and crabbed. I couldn't bear to leave it. They moved it by tractor – quite a labour of love, and for two years it looked as if it was dying, but since then it's gone from strength to strength. The berries have a lovely flavour – it's just like eating bumble bees."

As well as the changes brought about by the seasons, this garden is home to a zoological soap-opera nurtured by its owners, particularly in the wild hinterland of the river – strips of cloth soaked in fox-repellant form a pungent guard of honour to nesting swans. In some years, they lost all their eggs to marauding foxes, but more recently, they successfully reared young.

Some years ago, an enormous white goose suddenly walked through the garden gate and took up residence. A familiar carp twinkles from the water on a good day, and the bank has been shuffled bare by a badger pottering contentedly from a snack of bluebell roots: "He ruckles up the ground, I don't know why." Taking their cue from their owners, the Baths' dogs Rutty, a Rottweiler, and Maria, a King Charles spaniel, observe the wildlife on and around the river with benign tolerance.

Lady Bath is something of a miniaturist. The same fascination for detail that used to result in exquisite pencil drawings of flowers, now finds expression in her greenhouse. "I love my small greenhouse, it's a real joy. It's lovely to go out every day in winter and potter in there, especially in the evenings. It's like a little Aladdin's cave. I sit on the seat and really revel in it all."

Here are miniature Chinese gardens, with pensive tiny figures and bridges; carnations grown from cuttings snipped from bouquets; orchids which Lord and Lady Bath found growing wild in Peru. Lady Bath grows geraniums from seed: "It makes you feel so clever, though it's not at all." Her shelves groan with busy Lizzies and cyclamen: "Pygmy ones don't take long from seed."

Lord and Lady Bath are not young, but they are youthful. She has a girlish diffidence about the garden: "It's an eternal thing of forgetting what I should have done. Very Laurel and Hardy but not at all funny – when I'm planting bulbs I always find that I've dug into the most beautiful white thing that was just about to appear."

Her final remark was a thoughtful and appropriate generalisation: "Most people who have gardens have such a charm about them."

Above　*The Wylye, with the resident swan family*
Right　*The mill seen beyond the shelving lawns and topiary garden*

HUGH JOHNSON

*Judy and Hugh Johnson's garden at Saling Hall in Essex
is a rich and eclectic mixture of gardening styles, reflecting
the catholic and idiosyncratic interests of its creators*

Judy and Hugh Johnson first saw their house in September 18 years ago, and fell in love with it instantly. It was long and low, with pale pink and blue bricks, and Dutch gables. Five different vines which covered the front had turned a variety of golds and ambers, and carried heavy crops of ripe grapes.

Inside the walled garden, the walls of which are dated 1698, roses such as 'Gloire de Dijon' and 'Phyllis Bide' cascaded and rampaged over the old iron gates, bedheads and other Heath Robinson contraptions put there to support them. Over the years the Johnsons have replanted the walled garden beds, and ruthlessly ripped out the garish floribunda 'Masquerade' roses. "To achieve interest in the garden all through the year has been our main aim, and to divide the garden up into a series of small rooms, each with its own mood and character."

For many years Judy was looking after small children and driving them to and from school, so Hugh was the creator and inspiration for the planting. Luckily he paid little heed to those who advised against planting yew hedges, as being too slow – patience and gardening go hand in hand, especially as theirs is a garden with a particular emphasis on trees. "We no longer stand in

awe of those magnificent towering elms, as they all died soon after we came here. Instead, we drool over the new shoots of *Populus koreana*, the scented blossom of *Elaeagnus angustifolia*, and many coloured berries – all within easy reach; and occasionally we worry and agonize over sickly leaves or damaged bark."

When the full flush of summer is over, the peonies and agapanthus give way to softest pink and white Japanese anemones. The brilliant scarlet dahlia, 'Bishop of Llandaff', crowds out the alstroemerias, and the purple Michaelmas daisies echo the purple of *Buddleia* 'Lochinch'. Judy relishes this time of year. "Through the mist, on a perfect autumn morning, I can see the golden maple, *Acer japonicum* 'Aureum', with colchicums sheltering at its feet; and beyond it, *Acer hersii* and Japanese maple.

A large amelanchier, which turns a wonderful ruby-red at this time, but seldom has much blossom as the birds eat all the buds, gracefully shades a new bark garden. They have recently planted *Nandina domestica* 'Richmond', *Paeonia delavayi* and *Hydrangea quercifolia* there. "We are also planning to add to this area some *Camellia sinensis*, the tea plant, which we brought back

*Left   An Italianate, algae-covered staircase, in brilliant setting of autumn leaves
Above   Hugh Johnson contemplating serious labour with a leaf-rake
Overleaf   The handsome exterior of the house. A peaceful scene, in spite of the proprietorial swan*

from a trip to Georgia in the Soviet Union. When these mature it will be our 'Tea Garden'."

The Johnsons have a small waterfall tumbling over rocks, in the style of a garden in Kyoto, with *Fuchsia magellanica* 'Alba' and a dwarf pine, *Pinus mugo*, partly concealing the water. *Rosa rubrifolia*, which loves this garden and seeds itself everywhere, is covered in orange hips, when its little pink flowers are over.

In the next pond are reflected the dark grey bronze Shinto arch, or 'Tori', which they have recently installed, and the startlingly white trunks of *Betula jacquemontii*. On a warm sunny bank there is a collection of *Sorbus* in berry, *S. hupehensis* and *S. vilmorinii* being particularly good. Yellow berries, fortunately less popular with the birds, grace *Ilex aquifolium* 'Bacciflava' and *Cotoneaster* 'Exburiensis'.

A ride through a grove of brilliant yellow Norway maples passes the best of all autumn-colouring cherries, *Prunus sargentii*, and on to the water garden. *Gunnera manicata* grows vigorously all summer in these damp surroundings, and its leaves completely cover the first small pond. In the shade of the parrotia, liquidambar and swamp cypresses, the last few primulas vie with the irises for space.

In the walled garden different varieties of cooking and eating apples, such as 'Bramley's Seedling' and 'Ellison's Orange', have been treated almost as topiary, and for many years cut into mushroom shapes. They still crop well, but they are laborious to prune, and must be pruned annually. "These trees make the most wonderful natural parasols for lunching under on a hot summer day, and we don't have to go far to pick the salads, herbs and vegetables for lunch, as the next walled enclosure is the kitchen garden."

Here the Johnsons grow a wide range of vegetables, including asparagus, new potatoes, courgettes, and different varieties of lettuce: 'Little Gem', 'Salad Bowl' and 'Continuity'; also purslane, rocket, Pak Choi and a Japanese salad called 'Shizo'. In between the rows of broad beans and mangetout peas they grow marigolds, nasturtiums, dill and summer savory. A hedge of sweet peas divides the artichoke bed from the soft fruit cage where the late raspberries ripen in September, and from which Judy picks a magnificent crop of red and black currants.

In this walled garden, the path leads under an octagonal iron pergola covered with *Solanum jasminoides* 'Album', the Oregon thornless blackberry and the beautiful pale-lilac climber *Cobaea scandens*. When winter comes, the bare bones of the garden are more apparent – the sharp contrast of the young trunks against the dark greens of the pines, spruces, clipped box and yew. There is the smell of wintersweet, *Lonicera fragrantissima* and sarcococca, or Christmas box. Around the corner lies spring, and all the excitement of a new season and another hectic year.

Above   *A Japanese 'Shinto' arch, an Oriental touch emphasised by autumn leaves and bamboo*
Right   *Tranquil reflection of the startlingly white trunks of* Betula jacquemontii

COTTAGE GARDENS

MARY KEEN

*An apprenticeship on the National Trust garden panel
gave Mary Keen an approach to gardening both fastidious and
romantic – qualities that have led to a dual career
as author and garden designer*

Mary Keen grew up amid a garden laid out by Percy Cane, whose formal style was much sought after in the 1950s. But the wide, beautifully kept lawns, long herbaceous borders and ornamental pools never really appealed to her. "Far prettier, I thought, was the abandoned sunken garden where grape hyacinths and anemones pushed their way through the paving stones, or the banks of the Avon where fat clumps of primroses grew. I spent my early days lying reading in the long grass or doing too much riding, and it never occurred to me to want a garden of my own." Yet she must have been susceptible to flowers because one of her most vivid memories is of the kitchen garden at the school where she was a boarder.

"It was the summer term – I can't have been much more than ten – when I got out of my bed very early one day for a dare and stole around outside in my pyjamas. When I came back, I brought with me one of the 'Mrs Sinkins' pinks which lined the paths in the old-fashioned kitchen garden, and told my roommates how lovely it looked. It must have been beautiful because I still have an impression of that kitchen garden on an early morning in summer, while memories of ponies and the garden at home faded long ago."

After she married she was much influenced by her mother-in-law, a painter, embroiderer and gardener of no mean talent. Her mother-in-law suggested that gardening was something that could be combined with bringing up small children, and arrived to stay with Vita Sackville-West's books and trugfuls of plants from her own garden. Their first house was a rented vicarage (Victorian and very cold) in the Midlands with formal rosebeds, collapsing greenhouses, a pond and a vegetable patch. "We learnt to prune roses and grow vegetables, but we couldn't afford to heat the greenhouse and much of our time was spent trying to keep our small daughters from wandering too near the pond."

After a year they moved 50 miles north, and Mary gave up reading anything except gardening books. She read Vita Sackville-West, Graham Stuart Thomas, and Scott's and Hillier's catalogues over and over again. "I read them in the bath and while the children quarrelled, and I dreamed of the flowers I would grow." She planted 'Nuits de Young', 'William Lobb' and 'Rosa Mundi'; they grew more vegetables and had another daughter.

They moved again to another rented house, this time in Berkshire on the banks of the River Lambourn, with a derelict but ravishing garden where *Tulipa sylvestris* grew in the gravel and 'Zéphyrine Drouhin', the thornless rose, climbed the walls of the house. There were apple trees

Above   *Mary Keen at work, with a green view of Berkshire beyond a vase of fragrant
old-fashioned roses, and the ubiquitous 'Yellow Book' to hand*
Right   *Roses, geraniums and delphiniums in pastel, cottage-garden profusion*

and flat tiers of *Viburnum* 'Lanarth', and a little wilderness where foxgloves and peonies grew. She read Christopher Lloyd and discovered foliage, ordered *Mahonia lomariifolia* and a *Parrotia persica* (which wasn't suitable). "Then I woke early one summer morning, looked out of the landing window, and saw the garden and the river, damp and mysterious in the early dawn. I went down to weed the peonies, and it was like falling under a spell. That enchantment has never been broken."

A move back to the Midlands meant another intractable house to paint, and heavy clay soil to dig, after the Lambourn chalk. "This was my Margery Fish phase: hellebores and cottage plants and rather too much variegated foliage." But old roses remained a favourite, and the house had a narrow conservatory which provided a new sort of horticultural challenge. "Even after 12 years of indulging in what had by now become an obsession, I still made terrible mistakes." Trees that had taken a morning to plant were often dug up and moved a yard six months later.

Visits to other gardens occasionally had disastrous consequences: new beds, made on impulse after seeing an enviable layout, never turned out quite right. "This was the time when I started to look at other people's gardens, instead of just reading about them and cultivating my own. Garden history became an absorbing interest, and I began to realise that for a garden to be really successful it should be in the same time scale as the house."

They moved to their present home, a Berkshire rectory built in 1825, a dozen years ago. It had several fine trees, including an ilex and a walnut, and a view of a church on a green hill with a Scots pine in the hollow below it. There was a walled garden where chickens pecked, and honey fungus, ground elder and brambles everywhere. The only concession to a garden was a curved double border full of tired Michaelmas daisies and goldenrod, and a legacy of trees and shrubs planted in the 1950s, which were out of keeping with the matchless 18th century view. The *Prunus* 'Pissardii' in a straight line across the landscape behind a weeping willow obviously had to go.

"I wanted a secret, mysterious garden, the garden of my dreams and memories, but put together with the experience that comes only from making mistakes." There was much agonising over whether to shut out the view completely, but the final decision was to respect the genius of the place, and resist the temptation to plant anything in front of the house that would detract from the sweep of the green glimpsed below the church

tower. "I do not regret my choice: the magic of the view flanked by woodland is every bit as compelling as the memory of that kitchen garden or that early summer morning by the Lambourn." Everything on the south side of the house was designed to frame the view: pale flowering shrubs and evergreens, in clumps down the garden, edge the scenery of the valley like theatre wings. Some *Rhododendron ponticum* bushes, which were part of the old parsonage planting, were left because they make a good dark background to flimsier shrubs. Mary liked the feeling that they were solid old-fashioned shrubbery material, the sort that was always found around rectories and vicarages in the early 19th century.

"After so much trial and error in my own and other people's gardens I'm fairly sure that what matters is to make the best of what you have and to emphasise the character of the house, rather than to impose any kind of alien arrangement on it. Pope's advice to 'consult the genius of the place in all' remains the best guiding principle for a gardener."

After going through crazes for various types of plants she is still susceptible to things that she has never grown. She still fights the temptation to try everything because she has learned that the garden would end up looking like a collection of bits and bobs if she allowed herself a free rein. As she plans schemes for other people and works in her own small plot in London, there are always opportunities to try new things, "but in any garden what I like to aim for is the whole, a place which enfolds you in its own mood. I think I prefer those rather misty dream-like gardens where you wander slowly in a trance to the ones which are full of surprises and novelties. I don't like gardens which are too tidy; I like an atmosphere of abundance and of languorous scents; I want to walk slowly from place to place, lingering to look at a flower or a view. I like to sit on a seat and think about how it might look if I only did this or that, because I love the making of a garden so much better than the maintaining; the travelling hopefully, rather than the ordered completion."

In front of her house there are winding shrubberies, with simple flowers, including philadelphus, exochorda, *Rubus tridel*, species and shrub roses, as well as sweet briar; and evergreen viburnums, hollies, yew and plenty of box. Off the main axis of the garden, conveniently hidden by the fall of the land and a large walnut tree, is an inherited and rather broken swimming pool. It is now painted dark brown ("There is nothing so

awful as that flash of Hockney blue in the English landscape.'') and surrounded by dark trees and yew hedge. 'Wedding Day', 'The Garland' and 'Rambling Rector' roses clamber into the hollies to make a backdrop to the shallow end, and at the deep end there is the view of the green hill and the church.

At the back of the house is a kitchen garden, walled on three sides and hedged with a double row of beech on the fourth. Vegetables are grown here for the family, with old-fashioned flower borders which run along the central path under arches of pears and roses trained on iron hoops. A Gothick trellis-work summerhouse in the corner shelters pots of tender plants in the summer months. In this garden, bright colours face no competition from the view, and the borders are crammed with columbines, pansies, peonies, roses, poppies, delphiniums, sweet Williams, cornflowers, daisies and pinks. "Anything, in fact, that I like the look of, mixed in with the odd clump of rhubarb, artichokes when the winter doesn't kill them, and a few bushes of box and lad's love." It is totally different from the peaceful prospect at the front.

There is another small, enclosed garden at the back, where herbs grow in formal beds surrounded by brick paths and enclosed by box hedges. Here a seat, flanked by pots of lilies, catches the evening sun. Leading out of this and round to the terrace at the front is a tiny spring garden in the shade of some crab-apple trees and a solitary, purple-leaved *Prunus*. Roses follow when the early spring flowers are over – 'Cerise Bouquet'; *Rosa rubrifolia*, with dusky purple leaves; 'Paul's Himalayan Musk', and an extravagant honeysuckle that climbs to the top of a tree; this is the pale yellow etrusca which scents the whole garden in July. In the orchard behind these gardens, wildflowers grow, and there are paths cut through the long grass which is never mown until August.

"Now that the bones of the garden are laid, I want more embellishments; statues, better pots, even a grotto." She longs for the hedges and shrubs to grow to increase the sense of enclosure because, although they moved into the house over ten years ago, everything has had to be done in gradual phases.

"I cannot imagine a time when it will all be finished. The piecemeal approach is not the approved way to make a garden, but it is a style which suits those who relish the pursuit of the unattainable. I was lucky enough to discover the pleasures of gardening in my 20s; for most people it comes much later in life and by then it is often too late to start realising your dreams. 'English gardens', wrote Goethe, 'are not made to plan but to a feeling in the head.' Mine are always made that way."

A hammock slung invitingly between old apple trees in the front garden

SONIA COODE - ADAMS

*The grounds of Feeringbury Manor epitomise the
tranquil magic of Zen and the art of garden maintenance
for Sonia Coode-Adams and her husband Giles*

Giles and Sonia Coode-Adams both admire gardeners who are single-minded in their purpose, but see themselves as veritable butterflies. Like Gaul, they split into three: the garden designer, the plantsman and the wild gardener. When they arrived 11 years ago, the garden was a wilderness, a death-trap of hidden ditches, head-high nettles and a proliferation of tumbledown sheds which used to house their predecessor's chickens. There were seven or so acres of wilderness with no flowerbeds other than three circular beds of barely living roses, and a long border that had been conquered by bindweed and ground elder.

Faced with this prospect, their plantsman's instincts had to be kept under control and all efforts went into tidying the place up: removing sheds, wire netting and rubble, and then cutting the nettles and brambles, gradually replacing them with lawn. "Shortly afterwards we started the arduous job of planting the yew hedge, following to the letter Christopher Lloyd's instructions in *The Well-Tempered Garden.*" If you want a yew hedge behind a border you need to stop the roots invading the bed by digging a trench deep enough for a sheet of corrugated iron between hedge and bed. It was a back-breaking job but the reward

Above   *Giles, Sonia and their sculptor son Ben, on the terrace*
Right   *The river, a cool green summer retreat, dappled with elderflowers and fringed with rushes*
Overleaf   *The verdant exuberance by the top pond—once an impenetrable jungle of brambles*

after nine years is a fine hedge together with a flourishing border.

They dug the lower pond and made a stream down to the river, planting a short avenue of flowering *Malus floribunda*, which gives a shimmering mass of pale pink blossom in early May. Trees and beds were planted ferociously, paths laid and secluded sitting-out spots created. "Throughout the early years we were itching to handle the small, rare plants we had grown in our previous garden." With the making of the stream bed, this fantasy was at last indulged and they planted up this damp area with primulas, both blue and palest yellow meconopsis, the early white sanguinaria, creamy white Japanese *Kirengeshoma palmata* and a number of ferns.

"Apart from the unusual plants, we get a real thrill from many things that other gardeners might find dull or untidy. The cow-parsley flowering and stretching for acres on the opposite side of the river under the cricket-bat willows is a truly wonderful sight, particularly in the evening, when it has an ethereal quality. The buttercups, speedwell, wild violets and stitchwort in the hedge all lift the heart. Some will say this is not gardening, but it is and should be. We deliberately do not cut these patches and encourage wildflowers as much as we can – not always easy in our rich soil."

They have planted large numbers of lilies in the grass, some of which do well, mostly *L. tigrinum* and *henryi* varieties. There is a small woodland area where the year starts with snowdrops and aconites, followed by scillas, wood anemones and dog's-tooth violets (*Erythronium dens-canis*), and finishes off with daffodils, *Fritillaria imperialis* and blue camassias.

Later in the year the shrub roses come into their own; a long bed is filled to overflowing, with other roses in the mixed borders. Many clematis climb through them and prolong their season, along with wild sweet peas of crimson, white and the rarer, annual sky blue. Climbing roses, including the menace 'Kiftsgate', festoon the old fruit trees; the latter is forgiven its size when powdered with its white flowers. Other roses grown include the pink-tinged 'Francis E. Lester', 'Bobbie James' and 'Seagull'.

"Our main purpose is to achieve an element of surprise, like seeing a clematis in an unexpected but satisfying place; or small, hidden areas where you come upon a concealed stream or a seat. We try to avoid the feeling that the garden can be seen at a glance but try to keep it, if possible, slightly overgrown (though not with weeds) and to preserve an air of mystery." Some places are kept shady to heighten the pleasure of walking out into the sunlight.

Seeds and pots are not strong points; "We would love to have tubs of lilies and other rarities, but lack the time and concentration. Even winter bulbs elude us, though we enjoy seeing early-flowering hyacinths in other people's houses."

Vita Sackville-West condemned "a riot of colour" but Sonia admits that neither she nor Giles is keen on greenery and foliage. "We like lots of flowers and aim, in theory, to have the whole garden in flower all year round, though not at the cost of quality, which often means fewer plants but more interesting ones."

What of the future? According to Sonia, a finished bed is a dull bed, and luckily with frequent deaths there is always replanting to do. "The perfect garden would be extremely boring; in gardening it is better to travel than to arrive."

Left   *A cottage-garden mixture of dimorphotheca, campanula and Shirley poppies, dotted with scarlet Knautia macedonica, in dense profusion below the terrace*
Above   *The view over the top pond to the house, a 14th-century/Victorian hybrid*

MARGERY FISH

Margery Fish taught us to
look at plants afresh.
The reflowering of her garden at
East Lambrook is due to the
benevolent fanaticism of
Andrew and Dodo Norton

Fifty years ago, most people thought of cow-parsley as a weed, and had never heard of astrantia. The old primrose 'Garryarde the Grail' was thought to be extinct; and geraniums were, to most people's minds, scarlet, and spilled out of window-boxes. Margery Fish changed all that.

She and her husband Walter bought East Lambrook Manor in Somerset with some apprehension in the 1930s. The place was practically derelict, a desolate collection of farm-buildings, with no garden at all. Typically, it was the *Acer pseudoplatanus* 'Leopoldii' framing the front door that seduced them into buying the house. They started to garden tentatively in 1938, and from

Left   *Typically concentrated and mixed*
planting—cornus, mallow, alchemilla, roses and
euphorbia, with a topiary tree to give solidity
Above   *Margery Fish, held in affectionate*
remembrance by everyone who knew her
Overleaf   *No inch is wasted, and as soon as the apple*
trees can support their own growth, climbing roses
are trained up and over them

then East Lambrook evolved in all its subtle intricacy until Mrs Fish died in 1969. The architectural framework of the garden is of Ham stone paths and a cavalcade of fat clipped evergreens, known affectionately as 'Margery's humps' or 'pudding-trees'. Within this outline is an ever-changing profusion of plants.

The garden has a very thin layer of topsoil, covering a stratum of solid yellow clay. Mrs Fish soon realised that treading on the ground compacted the soil, so her wide borders are ribbed with regular, narrow pathways. Because of the inhospitable land, some plants don't grow as big as they might elsewhere, but the dominant impression is of happy abundance.

She did not like to see bare earth, and East Lambrook Manor garden is extraordinarily thickly textured. There are thousands of plants, and nothing is the obvious variety of anything. The first of over 200 forms of snowdrops flowers here in October. There are 120 old named primroses, including many that had been thought extinct. In June, there are 130 different kinds of hardy geraniums in flower. *Geranium pratense* 'Bicolor', or 'Striatum' is a typical rarity, delicate petals patched and striped with colour.

February is a colourful time in this garden, thanks to Margery Fish's collection of hellebores, thought to be one of the largest in Europe. There are more types of *H. orientalis* than you would

Andrew and Dodo dining alfresco under the
Acer pseudoplatanus *'Leopoldii' that began the*
whole saga in the 1930s

charm of dusty pink cow-parsley when most people were attacking it with scythes.

Margery Fish's generosity and sweet nature are legendary among plantophiles. Anyone who showed interest in a plant would end up with a basketful to take home. And now that Andrew Norton and his wife Dodo have taken on the Augean task of restoring this two acres of herbaceous petit point, they have been helped time and time again by the grateful recipients of Mrs Fish's generosity, who visit bearing baskets of this and bunches of that. "Plants became her children," according to Andrew, and like all happily brought-up children, her plants have a way of coming home.

Inevitably, after her death and without her original guiding passion, East Lambrook succumbed to the dominant plants, and the whole place became very claustrophobic. As Andrew says: "It was supposed to be a labour-saving garden, but actually it is the most labour-intensive garden you could imagine." He spoke with feeling.

The Nortons bought East Lambrook Manor in August, 1985: fortunately they fell under the spell of the unruly garden and have thoroughly enjoyed bringing it back to life. This followed a perfectionist's piece of horticultural archaeology. Some of the garden was engulfed in brambles and nettles, but the worst was the ground elder. A whole bed had to be cleared and left fallow, with its previous inhabitants kept happy elsewhere until the ground was declared safe. Everyone had to be very careful about clearing weeds – every leaf had to be examined, to make sure that it was not the last extant of a dwindling species.

The hundreds of slides that Margery Fish used to illustrate her lectures were catalogued and studied; together with her books, they showed the garden's development. The Nortons were helped enormously by the reappearance of Maureen Whitty, who had worked for many years in the garden alongside Mrs Fish.

The exuberant restoration of Margery Fish's garden is due to the energy, dedication and ex-military methodicalness that Andrew Norton and Dodo brought to it. They put back 3,000 plants in their first three years. Now the garden is reaching maturity again: "If you don't garden it intensively for a week, it has taken over".

It will never disappear again. Andrew is tabulating the particulars of every plant on his computer: "There is a database and 26 different fields of information on each plant. It would be terrible if this were all lost again." Given their affectionate dedication, it is most unlikely.

ever expect to see in a single garden, ranging from the purest white to darkest purple, with spotted, speckled and reddish forms in between.

At first Margery Fish's interest in flowers was as an arranger, and it might have been the close scrutiny of petal markings and leaf forms, as advocated by Constance Spry, that led to her fastidious plant choices at East Lambrook. Her taste was for subtle colours, delicate markings, strange seed-heads, the tiny and overlooked forms of more familiar flowers. She recognised the

DEBBIE WELDON

*A New York childhood and a glossy London
modelling career were unlikely preparation for
Debbie Weldon's present perfectionist
approach to her country garden*

As a young New Yorker, Debbie Weldon wanted to be a florist. One of the local flower shops had a constant curtain of water streaming down the plate-glass window; it diffused the outlines of the bold, fresh flowers into a dream of perfection. "At home I read Frances Hodgson Burnett's *The Secret Garden* and sang to myself from *The Waltz of the Flowers . . .* 'bleeding heart greets periwinkle . . .'. No one else in my family had any interest in horticulture, though latterly my sister has been obsessed with growing water-loving hydrangeas in baking Dallas."

In London, a modelling career kept her out of the garden, though the sooty city soil was not tempting. Her first house in the country was a farmworker's cottage in Hampshire. The garden area was about half an acre, but the only thing growing there was an old Dorothy Perkins' rambler. There wasn't even a lawn.

"I planted a row of blue hydrangeas under the 'Dorothy Perkins', which I interspersed with 'New Dawn', a vision of pink and blue. My new garden took in all my favourites: peonies, lilacs and delphiniums which grew to be giants. A young wisteria began to cover the wooden porch. Moving into a bare plot, there are no senior citizens to respect, so I had a blank canvas. It has taken me a long time to learn to move or discard old plants."

The soil in Hampshire was light and loamy, and the weeds came out of the ground at a touch. She only knew what she had read, and to make up for lost time, she would work until nightfall in summer. It was a high, open spot, filled with light for as long as it remained in the sky. After four years she moved on, but for a few seasons was asked back to prune the roses. "Leaving a garden is worse than parting from friends; they, at least can travel to see you."

Next was a large Georgian house in south Wiltshire. The picture of a cherished dream, a huge ropy wisteria covered the smooth, mottled stone façade. "From a 20-foot ladder stretched up to the guttering, I used to prune the wisteria back to five buds in August, three in December, and by mid-May I had to part the cascading flowers to get a clear view from my bedroom window."

On arrival, the flower beds featured thick bramble, dotted with discarded gin bottles. The soil cracked widely when the sun got hot. "Impatient, ignorant and stubborn, I disregarded the books, and without 'preparing a rich soil', shoved peonies, delphiniums and lilacs into isolated holes with just a handful of bonemeal, a little peat, and some mature manure. Surrounded by cracking clay, they grew wan and anaemic. Numerous failures taught me that you can't bully nature, and suitability of soil must be a cardinal rule. After seven back-breaking years, I moved on to my present home."

Here a third-of-an-acre strip is divided by the house which lies lengthwise along it. Sheltered from the north, the back hugs a steep bank up to woods behind, where rooks and crows return to roost at dusk, and the security of the tall trees brings many birds into the garden. When she

An attitude of uncharacteristic repose in a garden rescued from jungle by unremitting hard labour

moved in, the bank was overhung with laurel, dripping over the house like the trees in Snow White's forest. Her occasional outdoor man, Sean, pruned the laurel, flinging the residue over her boundary into the woods, and creating what for a while looked like a smart hedge, but now has become an inexhaustible supply of kindling.

The house is basic, built of white brick with a pitched roof and symmetrically positioned sash windows. The front door faces east, and the long side of the house, with most of the windows, faces south. The outlook spans 180 degrees across a valley of farmland to the church tower of Dunhead St Mary on the opposite hill. Breathtaking views are common in the Wardour Vale, but even locals suffer a sharp intake of breath on their first visit.

To the south, the ground falls away from the foundations to a tall hedge, which runs the length of the property. From the raised terrace, it is just possible to see over the top. In summer, the panorama is filled with repeat-flowering red roses. "Over the access, to the east, I have constructed a rather gauche trellis arch, which will be covered, the sooner the better, with a white 'Seagull' rambler and butter-yellow 'Lawrence Johnston' climber." Round the edges of the terrace are lavender, perovskia and santolina, growing in half a dozen beds. Yellow *Clematis tangutica* and the prolific *Rosa banksiae lutea* on the house, fuchsias and marguerites in stone urns on the parapet, and Old Wardour Castle in the distance, framed by the trellis arch, create a glorious image to cherish through the sharpest winter.

The west of the garden is shielded from the view by the hedge of privet, holly and hawthorn; a rhododendron the size of an oak gives woodland shade. Under it are mature, weeping camellias and two dozen late-flowering 'Just Joey' roses, a present to the former owner from her husband. Debbie would never choose to plant roses in such a mass, but they flower for several months, a full, strong bloom, in the most beautiful apricot, and need little attention.

The first time she saw the garden, it had the feeling of a secret, wild garden. She scared off a couple of adders, and the unmarked graves on the deeds to the property suggested a spiritual population.

"With the birds, especially crows, the snakes and the frogs and plenty of self-seeded plants, it seemed like a deserted temple in the South American jungle, and I longed for Stewart Granger at my side."

Deep in the wood above the house, on the hill which shields the house from the north-east wind, there was once a stone cottage, long gone, and Debbie thinks that it housed the mechanism to make the waterfall in her garden. The water is pumped by an electric motor to a small pool at the top of the bank, and runs nearly 30 feet down an irregular course of uneven rocks into a series of three pools. The first pool is home to the frogs; the second holds thousands of tadpoles, and a multiplying band of self-supporting goldfish occupies the largest. Here is given the chance to fulfil another childhood fantasy – waterlilies.

The last third of the garden lies to the right of the entrance gate. Identified as the "bottom garden", it is usually seen only at a distance. "My meticulous tending of flowers and shrubs seems indulgent; raised four feet above the road, and in view of passers-by, no one ever sits down there. A stone figure, encircled by irises and holding a birdbowl, stands in the middle, but there is no wildlife. The atmosphere is tamer, and nothing is allowed to grow there without my permission. There are lilacs, peonies, heathers and roses in formation on spotless ground."

Up on the hill near the boundary, she has made a walkway, a natural but easy path from one end of the garden to the other, which she calls the "upper Corniche", after the top road on the Riviera. There, two tall pines accommodate a hammock, and create the feeling of swinging out into space. The path is reached from one end by a rough stone staircase cut through a massive laurel bush. From the "bottom garden", broad slab steps go up to a bench.

"Of course there is never time to sit on the bench or swing in the hammock, because my attitude to gardening makes it harder than perhaps it need be. Each plant is an individual whose health and happiness lies in my hands. Space, food and water and the removal of dead matter are the keys to their well-being." This means snapping off spent blooms on shrubs, snipping dead-heads on roses, shearing off the tops of heathers and cutting back climbers. She also feels compelled to cultivate parts of the garden that could easily lie dormant. "I long to see a haze of herbaceous jumble and tumbling climbers, but I can't stop these hands from clipping, snipping and pulling. The bait is that every year is better."

Mossy rocks and a high waterfall, foxgloves and St John's wort combine in a peaceful wildlife haven

BETH CHATTO

Beth Chatto took a challenging site in Essex, and by following an instinct for appropriate planting, changed a whole generation of gardeners' perception of plants

For the first 20 years of their married life, Andrew and Beth Chatto experienced the ups and downs of a fruit-farmer's life. He ran the farm, and she helped where she could, learning a lot about handling apples, people and an income that fluctuated between good and bad. In 1960 they built a low, split-level house on the back end of the farm, tucked against a gravel bank overlooking a spring-fed hollow.

Farming and gardening in East Anglia are conditioned by long periods of drought: fine for cricket and ripening the harvest, but irrigation is essential for many crops, and faded khaki becomes the normal colour of lawns after June. The opportunity to make a garden in permanently damp soil, perhaps to make a natural pool or two, seemed like heaven. They had learnt quite a lot about plants in their first garden and Andrew had spent much of his adult life studying the origins of garden plants but this new project was a huge undertaking.

Thirty years ago, gardens were mainly planted with cultivars of plants such as roses, delphiniums and pyrethrums that have, over generations, been "improved", made larger or double, by the observation and skills of horticulturalists. Species plants – that is, plants as they are found growing naturally in the wild – were not so familiar in gardens. "From Andrew I learned to love species plants and I learned that plants grow and look better when they are grouped in similar condi-

tions in the garden to those in which they grow naturally. It amounts to common sense. Plants from hot, dry climates do not succeed if planted in cold, north-facing borders, while plants from cool, damp woodlands wilt and die if thrust into a bit of sun-scorched gravel."

Filled with dreams of an aromatic Mediterranean garden on their starved gravel slopes, and of vast sheets of bog primulas filling the hollow where they sank up to their knees in black silt, they began. "Without dreams, it would have been a daunting task; with them we progressed slowly, one step at a time, learning every day, feeling like pioneers pushing through a jungle, excited by every small achievement. Side by side with this we were running the farm, facing more downs than ups. Money drains out of land like water."

They reached the point where it had to stop. The farm had to be sold. Andrew was worryingly ill. Should they leave their new home and emerging garden, now seven years old? "No, I decided, we will keep a small area of land beside the garden and I will try to make a little nursery for growing plants."

More than 30 years previously, Beth had been a member of Colchester Flower Club and had been providentially jolted out of her role as housewife and mother of two small daughters by Mrs Underwood, the founder Chairman. Beth was sent off to give talks and demonstrations of flower arranging to newly formed clubs around East

Right   Beth Chatto, almost hidden by dense foliage, festooned with the orange flowers of flame creeper, Tropaeolum speciosum
Overleaf   Verbascum, allium, onopordum, clary and pinks in an eclectic and successful combination

Anglia. (During the war Beth had trained as a teacher, but had no formal training in horticulture.) For these meetings she took flowers and foliage from their first garden, much of it unfamiliar in those days. But the effect was always the same: "Where did you manage to find those unusual plants?"

The answer was not simple. Many had come from seed lists published by horticultural societies; some from more enterprising companies; but the greatest part by far had come from the garden of her good friend and mentor of 35 years, the late Sir Cedric Morris, painter, of Hadleigh, Suffolk. "The first walk through his garden gate led me into a love affair which transformed my life. I had stepped into the magical world of plants; plants without end, endlessly beautiful."

Cedric's garden was not conventional, carefully planned and contrived around a framework of trees and shrubs. Most of it was contained in an old walled kitchen garden with a few ancient pear trees and a medlar, as reminders of its past. No space was wasted. Every square foot housed a seasonal succession of unusual plants, making every visit rich with a new discovery.

"There were hellebores whose faces I had to tilt, as every one was different, irises with petals like reflected rainbows, soft clouds formed by aromatic grey-leaved plants, old scented roses and gold-laced polyanthus and primroses. Bulbous plants came and went like lilies of the field, mysterious fritillaries, globe-headed alliums, stately asphodels – all in sweeps and drifts mingled like crowds at a medieval fair. When I gasped in admiration and envy Cedric would say: 'Scatter the seed.' And I did, to discover for myself how he had spent years on his knees weeding among treasured seedlings. Today his plants live on in my garden and in the gardens of others. Every day they remind me of him."

As the nursery business developed, so did the garden, both in step, dependent on each other. With more help, more land could be properly prepared. One of Beth's peccadilloes is pride on providing employment on land that had not been previously cultivatable. "It would not have been economic to do the work we have done over the past 20 years in order to produce farm crops. At times I have been advised to sell it by visiting nurserymen when they saw the extremes of soil conditions. But over the years, I have watched my staff grow in enthusiasm and skills, well able to tackle the worst – and that we have done."

But unlike a painting, a garden is never finished, is never the same two seasons running. There is always change, and inevitably, decay. Courage is sometimes needed to strip away part of the old design, restore the texture and fertility of the soil, and then plan and replant another scene: perhaps a new combination of plants collected from the tiny bits of root, cuttings or seeds that find their way into the propagating house from friends, trips abroad or from visiting other nurseries.

"In the garden of our first married home I came to realise how much more I valued the overall effect of leaves than the fleeting colours of flowers. In that garden where drought was such a problem, grey-leaved plants clothed the garden for much of the year like background scenery waiting to be lit up by passing charades of colour. The garden never looked empty without flowers; patterns were made with different shapes, textures and colours of leaves. Now I have indulged this love of foliage to include all the great moisture-loving plants, such as gunnera, rodgersia, rheum and ligularia species, while hostas and ferns flourish in shady places."

Beth continued to worry until the winter of 1975. She was still not convinced that she had a viable business. One day, feeling particularly depressed, she met the local fishmonger, eldest of a family of fishermen from the village. "Don't you worry," he said, "you have something personal to offer, you stick to it. It took us eight years to become established." Today they are the only privately owned fish shop left in town, and the best. She went home encouraged and decided to take a small exhibit of winter plants to the Royal Horticultural Society Hall in Westminster. The weather had been mild. There were plenty of hellebores, ajugas and pulmonarias in flower, while the variegated foliage of London pride and honesty was just as colourful. "To my astonishment and gratitude the Press fell upon us with delight. I suspect they would have reacted as strongly if I had taken nettles, as they are ever on the lookout for something new."

As a result of her idiosyncratic taste, Beth Chatto's garden is an object lesson in the intelligent exploitation of a difficult challenge. Luckily, the gardening world has also benefitted.

A subtle mixture of glaucous colour, including edelweiss, a dark and spiny eryngium and allium

GERMAINE GREER

The originality and passion that went into 'The Female Eunuch', now finds expression in 3¼ acres of environment-friendly garden, orchard and woodland

Germaine Greer has lived for two years on the borders of Essex and Cambridgeshire, in a house which is an attractive conglomeration of cottages. It presents a fierce and flinty east wall to the road; its prettiest side looks south, onto the most established part of the garden she is making. Here she has a terrace, a lawn, and against a wall, a wide mixed border spilling onto a path of flagstones.

"I didn't know what gardens were until I saw England and Italy" she admits. In Australia, where she was brought up, the gardens were "hateful", with lawns of stiff buffalo-grass and drives edged with blue spruce, liquidambar, cypresses, and "absolutely horrible" hydrangeas.

The beginnings of her love affair with Italy are described in the introduction to *The Madwoman's Underclothes*, a collection of her essays. When she acquired her own house there, she carved a garden out of the brambles. "I scattered a packet of seeds called Mixed Border (Tall) and was astonished by fountains of border carnations." Her Italian garden is elderly now; "old rose bushes and travelling honey fungus. I should rip it all out but I can't bear to. The first rose I planted is there, and my cats are buried there."

Her family in East Anglia consists again of cats. A beautiful marmalade creature with eyes match-

The writer–gardener in a firmament of Michaelmas daisies

ing his fur is introduced as "Christopher Greer", plus "Parrot Greer", with a red tail. There is always a fluctuating number of visiting Australians and "people who need shelter". Germaine Greer is divorced and childless, but she says "we" more often than "I". She is a matriarchal householder, breaking off her conversation to check out the hilarity in the kitchen, where old sheets are being dyed in the washing machine.

She finds it impossible to think of any gardening writers who have influenced her, though she thinks one can learn from television programmes. Gardening "is not something learned at school". Perhaps it should be. She acknowledges having picked up a great deal from her friend Pam Clifford, who gave her a lot of plants and was the

first person she saw propagating from cuttings. "I'm trying to propagate the *Buddleia auriculata* that flowers in mid-winter. My trouble is I'm away so much, and always at the wrong moment." She's becoming something of a "black gardening writer" herself, complaining about the "callousness of nursery gardeners" who sell inferior plants knowing that you'll have to come back for replacements; and about the way stable manure sold to gardeners is full of seemingly indestructible wood-shavings instead of straw.

"I bought this house in a spirit of cynical detachment. I was disillusioned with London, and I can't live in my Italian house all the time – I can't work there." She needs libraries, and Cambridge is only 10 minutes away by car. "But

Above   *The ivy-clad exterior of the house, overlooking a border to be proud of.*
Right   *Germaine with Christopher Greer, a feline member of the family.*

already the place is winding itself around me. I had thought: 'I'll fit the house, not make the house fit me, and I'll do nothing in the garden for a year.' But as soon as I was in, I was peeling away the wallpaper and making plans for the garden." She didn't know, then, that she would be gardening on "builders' rubble and chalk, with sabre-toothed snails". Things die for no reason, perhaps, she thinks, because of quicklime. "We put on cartloads of manure, but we should have put on many more cartloads."

She has just over three and a half acres, and her plans are ambitious and long-term. At the moment, you need a visionary eye to appreciate them. "The idea is to have one acre given over to woodland, with a pond that we've already made. It's only a year old and it's full of life, but it's not right yet. It gets too deep too quickly." She took in someone "who needed shelter" who turned out to be a cousin of Alan Mitchell, the author of *Guide to the Trees of Britain and Europe*. "Gardeners are a special race of people. Alan drew up a plan for my wood with 200 trees, and gave it to me for free. I want my wood to be cover for birds and insects. I already look after seven beehives belonging to someone else."

Alan Mitchell told her that birds got bored by native trees, and put sumachs and Japanese maples at the front, for colour and variation. They seem to be flourishing, "though they hate chalk and wind. Until I lived here I didn't know the meaning of the word wind; it blasts and burns. We planted whips, very small trees, which was a false economy as all the rabbits in the area end up on my spit of land at harvest time. The trees should have been large enough to wear rabbit-bands to protect their trunks."

She intends to learn wood-management, she says, "by doing it". She means to introduce more *Daphne laureola*, hellebores, fritillaries, foxgloves, old man's beard and wild strawberries. "There will be room for one caravan in the wood for campers, and I'll be happy for people to come in and walk round the bark paths I mean to have, when it's all grown up in 20 years' time!"

The second acre, nearer the house, is a mixed orchard of apples, pears and medlars.

"We have the varieties that are going out of general cultivation specially grafted for us." This includes a local variety, called 'St Edmund's Pippin'. Germaine Greer is highly conscious of what is good to eat, whether for people or for wildlife. She has planted bullaces specially for the birds. She is equally conscious of what is poisonous, like henbane.

There is an old vegetable garden: "Raspberries and asparagus do well here, though we haven't yet mastered the management of asparagus." Cecil looks after the vegetables. "He's the Brassica King of the eastern counties." The only problem with Cecil's brassicas is the slowness and the smelliness with which the plants rot down. "I'm thinking of getting a shredder to speed the process up. I have a rolling compost system, with two piles, but people keep putting fresh stuff on the wrong pile."

For all her interest in trees and food plants, flowers and the insects they attract are her greatest love. "In Italy, I want to plant buddleias on a low terrace, and lie on a higher terrace taking photographs of the butterflies from above." It's complicated loving two gardens. "You do sometimes call them by the wrong name," she says.

Though gardening in Italy might seem to be more rewarding than in her problematic patch of East Anglia, she says not. "The climate in Italy is not as easy as you might think. My house lies in a horseshoe of hills, and the wind in November freezes the birds in the air. In summer, the sun is too hot, everything has set seed and gone by September. The season here is longer."

Meanwhile, her formidable vitality is transforming her English garden. "Maybe there is something female about gardening. Most of our traditional art forms are biodegradable and open-ended, not monuments to be preserved in museums. It's the same instinct that makes women twitch tablecloths and straighten curtains."

Metaphorically twitching a tablecloth, she expresses her current dissatisfaction with her planting scheme in the garden. "I want more narrow-leaved plants and aromatics, more mounds, fewer fronds. You have to be ruthless in order to be a good gardener."

URSULA BUCHAN

*Ursula Buchan, historian and horticulturalist, has written
a clutch of garden books, tends a Northamptonshire cottage garden,
and wins prizes for her sweet peas and vegetables*

For some children, a love of plants prompts them to grow cacti on bedroom windowsills, pansies in windowboxes, or rows of lettuces in the garden. These children often progress, in adulthood, to intense or even obsessive interests in gardening. Others, however, need an external stimulus to push them in the right direction – and so it was with Ursula Buchan.

"My mother was a very keen gardener, for whom gardening was a welcome recreation from the task of bringing up six children on her own. My horticultural efforts as a child were restricted to 'cutting the edges', of which there seemed to be a great many; one could hardly go wrong with a job which required only a certain tenacity."

Although raised with a strong notion that gardens were A Good Thing, in practice she found them a bore. While she absorbed unconsciously the names and ways of weeds, which stood her in good stead later on, and was given a rather ill-favoured little garden of her own where she grew spindly carrots and marigolds, it was not until after her mother's death when she was 15 that she became anything approaching a serious gardener.

"We children found ourselves bearing some unwelcome domestic responsibilities, which got in the way of the serious business of parties and enjoying ourselves, and the one that fell to me was that of looking after about an acre of garden.

"I detested the whole business at first. Hay fever reduced my sense of smell to almost nothing in June, so that I could not even properly appreciate the old-fashioned roses with which the garden was well filled, and gardening seemed to me to consist almost entirely of weeding. But I persevered, in a half-hearted way, till the day I saw the petals of a Madonna lily unfold. I was amazed at its pure whiteness and perfect trumpet shape and a little ashamed that, although these flowers had grown in a border all my life, I had never consciously seen them before." This intimation of how beautiful plants can be, coupled with a compulsion which stemmed from erratic fits of tidymindedness, sent Ursula to books to learn the theory and practice of gardening.

Her first self-appointed task was to prune the roses which had become almost overwhelmed with dog-rose suckers. They rewarded her efforts with a good flowering the following summer and she was very encouraged. At the same time the vegetable garden, which had reverted to a blissful state of nature, badly needed attention so she bought seeds and grew broad beans, leeks and herbs. "It was a revelation to me how simple growing was on this level and for some time I was haunted by the feeling that I must have missed the vital point somewhere. I seemed to have fallen into the beginner's trap of thinking it was all very easy."

A garden-minded friend gave her Vita Sackville-West's *Garden Book*. This was the first gardening book Ursula read for pleasure and it taught her that gardening, as opposed to mere maintenance, could be a source of great enjoyment even for people who had little aptitude or understanding. She caught a glimpse of what sophisticated gardening was and realised that her overweening confidence might have been a little misplaced.

Ursula Buchan, ready for gardening, with a defiant early spring blaze of Fritillaria imperialis
and tulips in the background

"I was fortunate, in a way. Circumstances had forced me to become a gardener earlier than is usual so that, after leaving Cambridge with a degree in modern history, I was able to make the mental leap necessary towards considering a career in horticulture. It occasionally struck me that it was a peculiar thing to have done, for I felt I was ducking the serious business of finding a suitable occupation and earning a sensible living." But she encountered no opposition; indeed she was positively encouraged.

A life as a professional gardener came to seem a most agreeable prospect and so, after six months in private gardens in Oxfordshire, she spent a year at the Royal Horticultural Society's gardens at Wisley. After that came some months with the bulb firm of van Tubergen in Haarlem, Holland; a spell in one of the great European arboreta at Kalmthout in Belgium; and, finally, three years as a student on the Diploma of Horticulture course at the Royal Botanic Gardens, Kew.

"When I look back now, that journey towards becoming a trained gardener was fraught with difficulties and the ever-present possibility of an abrupt dead-end: if Wisley had not taken me on or if Kew had been suspicious of a history graduate, it might all have come to nothing." She feels that it says much for the authorities' broad-minded approach that she survived to become a bona fide gardener, and it says something for the arrogance of the 20-year-old that she never antici-pated failure.

Her childhood expertise in edge-clipping came in very useful at Kew where, it has been estimated, there are 40 miles of lawn edges. "I am sure I cut most of them – when I could be dragged away from the pleasures of dumper-truck driving." After finishing her course she settled in a village on the limestone of north Northamptonshire, in a cottage with a half-acre garden of good light loam, fertile but sharply draining in summer.

The garden is dominated by a large and stately walnut tree which, though elegant, casts heavy shade. The garden slopes to the north, is open to the easterly winds, and shaded from the west by a neighbour's buildings and trees. Not the most auspicious conditions, but no gardener is truly contented with his or her lot or fails to point out the difficulties, the better to emphasise all the achievements.

"The circumstances in which I now find myself, along with my slightly idiosyncratic career, have served to shape what some might call, a great deal too grandly, my philosophy of gardening. The whole point of gardening is that it should be enjoyable. That may sound blindingly obvious but it is remarkable how many of us see gardening in the same light as people in the 18th century saw leeching – as a self-inflicted but necessary wound, disagreeable but to be endured for one's ultimate benefit. Gardening should never be a hardship."

At the outset she believes a rigorous choice must be made concerning how the garden may best be enjoyed. For some, that choice consists of only mowing the lawn and filling the beds with labour-saving shrubs and groundcover. For others, it means breeding show chrysanthemums or air-layering magnolias.

"For me, the pleasure is contained in striving for a unified garden picture composed of a wide range of individually attractive plants, and in the refining of my practical expertise, but I recognise that these are not necessarily desirable ends for everyone. The garden should, after all, reflect its owner's personality."

Time is for most people a precious asset and the Micawber principle applies as much to the hours spent gardening as to the management of money. If one spends only that time, or less, which one has freely to give the result is happiness. If one spends only slightly more, the result is total misery.

She concurs with Kipling who wrote: "Gardens are not made/By singing: 'Oh, how beautiful!' and sitting in the shade". For Ursula, the attributes of hard work, wholeheartedness and dedication are as important in gardening as in all other inessential activities.

"I have learned not to set myself unattain-able targets; for happiness is, after all, most readily achieved when results equal or exceed expectations. If I aspire to a Sissinghurst, I know I will have to work for it. But if my children persist in using the lawn as the next best thing to Brands Hatch, I shall ignore without any feelings of guilt all the excellent advice on offer about spiking, raking, fertilising, weedkilling, scarifying and top-dressing."

She feels that everybody, whatever his or her aspirations, should make a plan: some idea of size, shape, colour and season must guide all planting. This is especially true for those who have taken over an established garden as she did. "Until I found the energy to do something about it, I annually regretted the orange lilies flowering among the magenta roses."

Having worked in gardens that have success-fully outlived their original owners, she advises everyone to plant at least one thing for the long-term, however small the garden or short the

tenure, and not to sacrifice all for the instant or immediate effect. "They will know a far greater excitement when, after several barren years, the magnolia or chimonanthus finally condescends to flower, than anything afforded by forsythia or winter jasmine." And she tries not to neglect peonies and irises, which, though their glory may last only a few days, emphasise the seasonal nature of the garden in a way that potentillas or floribunda roses do not.

"I have, at long last, learned the folly of planting what does not suit my soil or climate. Reared in the favoured gardens of southern England, I am putty in the hands of Cornish nurserymen who easily persuade me in their catalogues to buy *Clianthus puniceus* 'Albus' or *Convolvulus cneorum*." A succession of hard winters finally cured her, although she cannot rule out renewed addiction when next she visits a southern garden.

As a result of the distractions of small children, the pleasure of gardening has come to mean doing essential tasks and abandoning the time-consuming peripherals. "I try to avoid dissipating my energies, never as considerable as those apparently possessed by other writers whose talk is all of worm-killing and shrub-pruning, spraying and top-dressing, burning and disinfecting."

In early autumn she is quite content if she can see all newly delivered plants secure in the still-warm ground. Bitter winters have taught her how much safer plants are in the hospitable earth than left to wither in frozen pots. She sprinkles liberal amounts of sulphate of potash around roses and shrubs to toughen up their wood before the onset of winter, and wraps the stems of tender plants in straw and hessian or plastic sheeting. All the cleaning and clearing in the world will hardly seem worthwhile in the spring if half the plants are browned or dying. "Once that is done, I can relax and enjoy my garden both in retrospect and in expectation of a future of infinite and, as yet, uncompromised possibility."

The RHS gardens at Wisley, where Ursula worked as a gardener

DANA WYNTER

*In total and salutory contrast
to the glitzy life of Hollywood,
Dana Wynter, actress and writer,
now lives and gardens in the
peaceful green backwaters of the
southern Irish countryside*

On coming to Ireland, Dana Wynter was immediately struck by the differences between this country and everything she had ever known in England. "Everyone, including the farmers, has a decidedly laid-back attitude towards both their land and gardens; haphazard is putting it mildly. My unavoidable impression of Ireland is that the whole country looks like a naughty boy's bedroom: bits and pieces flung everywhere, oddments tucked away into corners or left to languish and be stepped over."

It is surprisingly easy to relax and fall into this happy-go-lucky mode; she soon realised that there's more to life than being disciplined and growing things in prim, school-marmish straight lines. "It's a matter of outlook, I suppose. Irish gardens epitomise their owners' generosity and naturalness. Making a grand impression is not high on their list of priorities – 'no bother to it' is the expression we use here."

Home is at the head of a five-mile glen carved by glaciers some 10,000 years ago, and within sight of a magnificent 350-feet high waterfall feeding a peaty-coloured stream, populated by small brown trout. The sides of the valley are covered with trees and most of the rocky slopes have tiny waterfalls; in winter, the whole glen can shimmer when cool sunlight is refracted from little frozen cascades.

*Dana, against a breathtaking backdrop of five miles
of tree-lined glen*

"When I built the house I used local stone, granite and mica-schist, working around the lone chimney which staked my first intention to this land." The original error of thatching with fragile oaten-straw was eventually rectified when the roof was stripped away, and replaced by sturdy Wicklow-grown reeds, a perfect solution but hell on the garden. Roses had to be savagely cut back, clematis disentangled from the rafters, and precious lavender bushes were crushed by the thatcher's mis-step on descent from his ladder. Ultimately though, it was worthwhile and the house is now accepted as part of the general habitat by local wildlife.

"Sika deer graze by the river, a heron comes and goes, and each morning two magnificent wild pheasants present themselves, hungry for breakfast. Without fail, one arrives on the dot of 5 am, the other 50 minutes later. After eating they go off in opposite directions; I'm convinced they're father and son. The farmer neighbour finds the young red foxes and the occasional mink less beguiling than I do, but then he has hens. We also share an ambivalence about the rather nice chunky

Above   *Looking down on the house, its roof, thatched with local reeds, barely visible above the greenery*

Right   *The house, though newly built, looks ancient. A floriferous tapestry of roses and lavender adds to this impression*

badgers. His nervousness stems from an unproven fear concerning their reputation for transmitting tuberculosis to his cattle, while I try to be charitable about the chaos and upheaval caused in the garden by their tunnellings after plants, roots and bulbs."

It's all part of living in the country, sharing the environment with hide, scale and feather without imposing human values. And every time the wood-pigeons decimate the young cabbage plants, and hares eat more strips off the young apple trees already buffeted by the fierce wind which blasts down the valley, Dana reminds herself of this. "It's better to avert your gaze when a kestrel plummets to rise in triumph with its small victim, lunch for the young nesting over in the rocks: better to think about planting a rowan tree on the other side of the river to match ours and the bliss of slinging a hammock between them for future grandchildren to watch the little trout rise to a fly below."

Dana calls herself an extremely impatient but lazy gardener; when drawing up her garden plans, the crucial decision is one of basic timing: "Not for me the promise that something will bloom profusely in three or four years' time. I want them now." The nurseryman at the Powerscourt Garden Centre knows that biennials are absolutely out. If she had realised that the fragrant philadelphus takes a couple of years to flower, she might have given it a miss – "on second thoughts, no I wouldn't; mock-orange is a must in my life, bringing back memories of Berlin gardens and the perfume of orange groves in California."

When deciding, many things have to be taken into consideration: a windy glen at 900 feet; peaty-acid soil; the beautiful and ever-present bitter-yellow gorse and broom against grey, granite stone walls; and the wild yarrow, in the same biting-yellow, seen against fox-gloves, heather and rhododendron.

She wanted all the colours to be in that spectrum; the plants had to be those that might grow here naturally. "I wanted the house to blend in, to be a completion of, rather than an intrusion on, my farmer neighbours' kinship with the glen." The place is now hidden by spruce,

larch and birch, the driveway curves down from a farm gate and cattle-grid which is more challenge than obstacle to the innumerable mountain sheep. And in the bowl formed by the crook of the driveway Dana has planted a variety of successively blooming heathers, white- and red-currant bushes, pale rhododendrons and a scattering of the feisty pink roses which clamber over forlorn beach-cemeteries in the west of Ireland.

There's an ongoing battle with the wind over various clematis which she keeps picking up from the ground and re-attaching to the walls of the house. Honeysuckle is more tenacious and the roses, strangely, are the best at holding their own. Even snow and ice don't kill them, or the mallow which is so generous with its pink flowers.

Past the final curve are the courtyard and the front door, where two mystery beds contain mock orange and flowers from seeds scattered too long ago to remember what was in their packets. Yellow-green hops climb a corner of the house wall. "Each year they are cut right back to the ground, only to reappear towards the end of spring and race up over door and window with such vigour that I can imagine the day when the place will be tied all round with hop-vines." The courtyard side under guest windows contains lavender and flowering tobacco plants, along with tiny alpine plants set among granite stones. Pink climbing roses are encouraged to spread their branches along with white clematis.

There is buddleia for the butterflies; and prolific *fraises de bois*, given to Dana by the same friends over the mountain who donated the hops, show their tiny white blossoms before the fragrant, sweet berries appear. Among them all grow sun-yellow Welsh poppies, weeds to the purist but providing an especially welcome burst of bright colour on misty, overcast days.

So it goes; a garden filled with fond memories, with slips from friends, various cuttings purloined on her travels, a mystery plant from the magnificent garden at Beaulieu, originally a gift from the Dame of Sark some years ago. As Dana explains, "It's a garden of reminders, of family in Zimbabwe and friends all over the world, of good intentions and lost opportunities."

VICTORIA GLENDINNING

*A fascination with plants began
with a childhood vision of Oriental poppies,
pansies and cherry blossom*

Victoria Glendinning admits to being an obsessional gardener, but not a very professional one. "My garden is neither large nor grand, and the names of plant varieties fly out of my head as knowledgeable questions form upon visitors' lips. Nevertheless, when I talk about my gardening, I am talking about a love affair. It's a late love affair. For years a garden was, to me, just a place where you saw flowers on the hoof, so to speak, though my lust for them began precociously early. I don't know whether all small children see colours with psychedelic intensity; but until I was about six it was like eating with my eyes. I fell out of a tree, landed flat on my back and, winded, opened my eyes to clustering masses of pink cherry blossom against a blue sky. That was the first dazzlement."

In the summer, she was transfixed by scarlet Oriental poppies with black centres, their floppy heads on a level with her own. "I floated the petals in a bowl of water: vermilion silk boats." There were also pansies in that first garden; some, hot dark velvet with yellow patches, others a flat cool blue. She remembers squatting eye-to-eye with these giants, totally absorbed by their vivid faces.

Smell and taste were exaggerated as well. There was a stray pink rose in the vegetable patch, to which she returned again and again, enjoying its warm, strawberry scent. There was the first-ever pear, picked out of the grass under the tree, as perfect and seductive as the forbidden fruit which Eve gave Adam in the garden of Eden.

Then it was all over, for years. When she married and had a garden of her own, it never entered her head to change it, or to buy plants. "I took both the design and the contents as something that came with the house, like the worn but still useful stair-carpet." They moved often and some gardens, like some stair carpets, were better than others; with four sons, "better" tended to mean better for use as a football pitch.

"The only contribution I did make has become a ritual. We moved to a rented house in Southampton with a back garden full of old trees. I bought some daffodil bulbs, at random. They turned out to be the kind with ghost-pale blooms which make other long-trumpeted bright yellow varieties look coarse. Magic in the long dark grass under the trees, they were the variety 'Brunswick'." She has planted pale daffodils in every subsequent garden, and they still exert the same fascination.

She only started to focus properly on gardening when the children began to grow up. She and her second husband acquired a weekend cottage by a pond in north Hertfordshire. It was exceedingly small, and the garden equally modest. The advantage of a tiny garden is that it can be packed with plants, creating a look of luxuriance for an outlay that in a larger area would need proper costing and design. "But I made mistakes even there. My spring garden was delicious; the roses (the wrong roses, but even so) carried us through until late July; from then until the end of the year all was desolation."

She now makes an effort to forget the spring, which in a well-established garden looks after itself very nicely, and disciplines herself to plan

Victoria behind the potting shed, in her variegated boots

for late summer and autumn. Part of the difficulty is that she dislikes chrysanthemums and dahlias, except for single white ones. "I like anything pale and daisy-shaped or starry, and let the herb (or weed) feverfew seed itself where it will." She thinks that Japanese anemones, which come in white and pink, are marvellous late-summer plants.

She was surprised to find that being a gardener means that you come to hate certain plants. "If I hadn't found it out for myself, I would have learned it from Vita Sackville-West, who said that ruthlessness was one of a gardener's essential qualities. One of the reasons why I'll never be a really good gardener is that I haven't even got the courage to eradicate the giant-sized evening primroses that shoot up all over my present garden, ruining my schemes with their leaning towers of silky yellow, and I'm too hostile to stake them."

Vita, who, with her husband Harold Nicolson, was the creator of the gardens at Sissinghurst, wrote in her influential *Observer* column: "I hate, hate, hate 'American Pillar' and her sweetly pink companion 'Dorothy Perkins'" and these two rambling roses were wrenched from their innocent beds all over Britain. "The only rose I really hate is the puce-coloured thornless climber 'Zephyrine Drouhin', which we planted in front of the cottage. She clashes rather horribly with the lavender-blue clematis 'Lasustern' which we put beside her, but then she clashes with everything."

A few years ago they moved house, pushing their belongings in the wheelbarrow along the edge of the pond, to a larger cottage next-door-but-one, with a larger garden. They enjoy seeing their former garden maturing under someone else's care.

"What I haven't told the newcomers, because they could hardly be interested, is that the 'Black Knight' buddleia at their gate comes from a cutting made by my father in his Essex garden; that the sage bush by their path started life in Hackney, the original slip given to me several years ago by the writer Michael Trend when we were both editorial assistants on *The Times Literary Supplement*; or that the spreading pink knotweed (*Polygonum bistorta*) comes from a scrap filched by me from the gardens of Exeter University when my second son was a student there. I could go on and on." Gardens become repositories of journeys, friendships and phases: visual documents of their owners' biographies, which no one else can decipher.

She has learned that you can impose yourself on a garden only to the extent that the soil, the climate and the site will allow. The soil of the present garden is chalky; the front garden, sloping down to the pond, is a frost pocket in winter, and shady from afternoon onwards, even in mid-summer. It is much colonised by ducks, who lay their eggs in the hedge-bottom. The back garden is another country: it dries out quickly, has only one shady border, and the south-facing beds, backed by a high wall, get very hot. Victoria has planted non-hardy cistus, hebe and ceanothus there, among the delphiniums that were there when she arrived.

"Plants get squatters' rights in my garden. Left to itself, the whole place would fill up with Canterbury bells, marguerites, foxgloves, daylilies, small nameless violas, purplish opium poppies and, of course, evening primroses. These are the indigenous populations, endlessly prolific. The most recent immigrants, introduced by me, tend to be blotched or striped. I am going through a phase of wanting variegated foliage, particularly the sinister, spotty-leaved pulmonaria, and variegated buddleia and weigela. When in doubt about a difficult corner, I fill it with another dogwood, *Cornus alba* 'Elegantissima'. It has plum-red stems and airy green and white leaves that develop pink streaks in late summer, wonderful with the setting sun behind them." Even her gardening boots are variegated. They are old wellingtons which belonged to one of the children and were once sprayed silver for a school play. The silver is now flaking off in patches, giving the boots a curious mottled effect.

"Another reason why I'll never be a really good gardener is that I think of leaves and flowers before I think of shape and form. I had to consider those things when we took over our present garden; there was just a large square lawn at the back, with a narrow border all round. Ambitiously and wildly, I started cutting into the lawn with a spade as if it were pastry, creating a swirling shape, and more space for planting. I'm still at it. I stand at the bathroom window, which affords an overall view of the garden, and, as I clean my teeth, notice a curve that is irregular, or too mean, and out I go again the next day.'

As a result, the lawn gets steadily smaller and the planting areas gets bigger; but then so do the plants, which is fine by Victoria. The, as yet unachieved, aim of the curving lawn is to convey to the eye that the garden continues in an L-shape not apparent from the house.

"We acquired the leg of the L-shape quite recently and until we got to know Bill, it was just so much waste ground. I first met him leaning over

the rail of the pond. He told me he had lived in our row of cottages as a child, before they were modernised. Life in those days, he said, was different. I waited. He spoke: 'In the old days, you see, you had your spring, your summer, your autumn and your winter.' I waited again, respectfully, to hear what it was we had now instead. But there was no more, apparently, to be said."

It was only recently that Bill, appalled by the neglected state of their new strip of garden, offered them his services and hand-dug the lot, which involved the eradication of battalions of nettles. It was then that Victoria learned about Bill's bonfires.

"This is the only useful information I have to pass on and it is Bill's. He gets his bonfire going nicely in the normal way, and then smothers it with whatever garden rubbish he has to hand. This makes an igloo-shaped mountain from which no smoke or flame can escape. It burns from the centre, and the igloo sinks lower and lower. More rubbish can then be added, and when the rubbish runs out, Bill takes spadefuls of earth and douses the smoke with that. By the end of the day, all that is left is a small mound of ashes and burnt earth." The neighbours have not been annoyed by smoke and the ashes mixture, once cool, goes straight back on the flowerbeds.

"Scented pink roses still intoxicate me: my current favourite is 'Celestial'. I still like pansies, though I cannot see them now with the surreal vision of a four-year-old. I still love flamboyant Oriental poppies, though I prefer the albino 'Perry's White'. Suburban planting schemes, and the shrill propinquity of laburnums, have spoiled pink cherry blossom for me, but we have planted a hawthorn by the back gate. Pears no longer seem to taste of paradise, and the only pear tree we have is *Pyrus salicifolia* 'Pendula', a lovely drooping grey-leaved thing with inedible fruit. But I am hooked now, and will be out there in my variegated wellingtons, exercising my imperfect skills on my imperfect garden, for as long as I can hold a hoe."

Spring at Sissinghurst, inspiration for countless gardens

WORKING GARDENS

TERENCE CONRAN

A sense of tradition and an eye for design has always characterised the creations of Sir Terence Conran: his fastidious and functional walled vegetable garden is no exception

You don't have to be with Terence Conran very long to identify some of his ruling passions. One of them is for vegetables, "more beautiful than flowers", and another is for "the next thing", whatever that may be.

In his airy London office above Heal's and Habitat lies a rectangular carpet, which he uses as a chart to explain the layout of Barton Court, his Oxfordshire home: "The house is here, the walled gardens are here, flowers for cutting are in a border here, the river is down here . . . ."

After a while, as he talks and prods and points, not only the plan of the place but every detail of form, colour and level begin to compose themselves on that carpet, clearly visible to the inner eye. "Perhaps," he says, a glint in his eye, "I should have a carpet specially woven, a panorama of Barton Court."

He has owned Barton Court for 15 years. "It was terrible at first. The house had been a school, and then more or less unused for ten years, but it still smelt of chalk. I bought it for the river that flows in front, and for the fantastic walled gardens behind. There was literally not one flower in them, just Christmas trees and masses of thistles."

Terence and Caroline Conran have altogether

Cigar in hand, and with a well justified beam of pride, Sir Terence Conran gives his vegetables a good soaking

20 acres of gardens and park. "There was a slope from the house to the river, but it was imperceptible – it looked like a flat field. The first thing I did was to build a raised garden in front of the house, supported by brick and flint walls like the battlement of a fortress, with a ten-foot drop on the river side. The house looks more settled now, as if it has always been connected to its garden and has grown up out of it – but people thought it was pretty peculiar at first. I had to send cars round to the other side, so what was the back of the house is now the front."

The main flower garden, the herb garden and the place to sit out and shell the peas are all in the raised garden. "The soil of the Kennet Valley is very gravelly and acid, so we add tons of compost and manure. The house was built in 1772 by the man who was constructing the Kennet and Avon Canal, it was his site-hut really. There was a lot of reconstruction in 1882, but we knocked most of that down."

This is the first major garden Terence Conran has designed; before that, he had a London garden near Regent's Park, and a tiny Suffolk cottage garden. "If you are interested in the way a house looks, you have to be interested in the garden as well. I think of it in the same way: shapes, colours, vistas, hazards and surprises. We have some very, very large Greek oil jars. You can see one of them, a vast pregnant pot eight feet high, down by the river, at the end of a long vista right through the house from way out the other side."

The only bedding plants he uses are lots of blue petunias massed in pots and tubs. "It's easy to make even a small garden look terrific if you have an architectural framework, with paths, slabs, tubs, and climbers up the walls." He is pleased with his present 'backyard garden' in London, which is planned around two brick circles. "It's an absolutely wonderful microclimate: everything grows and grows; the walls are completely and totally covered." (He is an expansive man. "Absolutely", "completely" and "totally" are his favourite adverbs. This may be the secret of his success.)

He loves French gardens, but the one personal influence he acknowledges is that of an aunt, Mrs Knowling, "who went collecting in the Himalayas, and had a famous garden in Devonshire where I stayed during the war". With his liking for old roses, climbers, grey-leaved plants and lavender, Conran is a classically good gardener. Fifteen years on from clearing the thistles, the garden is mature. "It took 12 years to establish. Now it's acquiring character all by itself: even the new walls have lichen on them.

"Perhaps the best moments are in early spring, when we have a total carpet of snowdrops under the trees, followed by a sea of small pale narcissi. We inherited these, like the wisteria on the front of the house. For a week in summer the façade is totally blue with it, and the roses are out at the same time."

The vegetable garden is at its peak soon after that. "We grow more than one sort of everything; lots of different kinds of potatoes and cabbages, spinach, courgettes, mangetouts, beans, artichokes, everything. It all happens at once. For a few weeks in the summer I could supply half the county of Berkshire! We give loads away, and freeze a lot, but then somehow no one ever wants to take anything out of the freezer. I bring a lot of stuff up to the office, so much that in the end nobody wants it: 'Oh, not more lettuces!' I'm not very well planned for late summer, and I'm always surprised at how everything goes on. We have an alley of cordoned apples with wild strawberries beneath them, which looks wonderful."

Caroline Conran is the one who takes the most interest in flowers. Terence Conran's heart is with his vegetables. The garden has been open to the public only once. "Caroline arranged it without telling me: thank God it rained and only four people came. I don't really like showing anyone round – except I am apt to say, 'Come and look at the vegetable garden', which surprises them."

The most famous vegetable garden in Europe is at the Château de Villandry in Touraine, between Chinon and Tours. It is a perfect reconstruction of a 16th-century *potager*. In this great walled garden the plots are divided up geometrically, edged with box and rose-covered lattice, and filled with all the vegetables known to French gardeners and cooks of the period: virtually everything that we have today, except potatoes. Conran's half-acre walled garden of vegetables is "laid out like a miniature Villandry, divided up with little paths edged with box or cordoned fruit, with an umbrella of four plane trees in the centre where the paths join".

Another walled garden is an orchard, with hens and geese; there is also a conservatory, and a screened swimming pool. There are melons and cucumbers in cold-frames, two large fruit-cages, vines ("not very good grapes") and tomatoes growing under glass. Caroline has filled one greenhouse with olives and mimosa, "a miniature Provence", and another is for houseplants and orchids. The Conrans do not show their orchids, or anything else, for that matter: "It's not on that

sort of grand gardening level."

All the work is done by "two young lads and someone to cut the grass. The lad in charge is a 22-year-old punk with blond hair and ear-rings; he has done a fantastic job in the vegetable garden – not a weed to be seen." With everything so well established, so "set and settled", only the trees present a problem. "My arrival co-incided with Dutch elm disease, though the elms that came down seem to be growing up again, and healthily. Most of the trees are over 200 years old – we have a beech-tree copse, and a typical country-house cedar tree – and they only

have about 30 years more of life." So they must plant for future generations. "I'd probably find it difficult to begin all over again somewhere else now. I don't think you can start a new garden much over the age of 40."

That's the bad news. The good news is that in the next breath Terence Conran is talking – total-ly, absolutely, enthusiastically – about the "even more ambitious" garden that he and Caroline are in the process of creating at their house in Provence. It is a matter of constructing terraces, building stone walls, and doing "wonderful things with water . . . ."

The perfect walled vegetable garden, well established after many years, with a neat formation
of plane trees in the middle

JESSICA HOUDRET

*A fondness for herbs developed into a thriving business
for Jessica Houdret, as a result of which she now
teaches, writes and provides the photography for her books*

In 1982, Jessica Houdret had just completed her university course, and had a horror of being shut in an office. The light, well drained soil of Farnham Royal where she lives is perfect for growing herbs, so she set up a small business selling plants and a delicious variety of scented things. "I was always interested in herbs. I visited other businesses and gardens. Rosemary Verey's garden is just wonderful. Her vegetable garden, based on Villandry, is a very beautiful little potager. Mine is an even more miniature version of that."

Jessica has one and a half acres under cultivation, in small manageable areas. "I haven't got box hedges because of the work. They have to be clipped twice a year. And the old-fashioned things like hyssop and wall germander are even worse. I've just got brick paths and divisions. The path is edged with pot marigolds and there are thyme, parsley and broad beans interspersed with summer savory along the edges of the beds. Herbs can be very untidy and rampant, and formal herb beds provide a lasting discipline and structure. They look so lovely, but you have to keep clipping them."

In the handsome outbuildings of her seventeenth century house she sold great tureens of pot pourri, and the separate ingredients for people to make their own – lemon verbena and rose petals by the sackful, essential oils, even pretty bowls to put it all in.

Roses, scented flowers and herbs have been used for centuries to sweeten the air and mask less pleasant smells. In Roman times, Nero covered the floor with rose petals and provided great banks of them on which his guests could lie. Jessica's research has revealed that the eccentric emperor Heliogabulous went one step further: several of his dinner guests actually suffocated from the excess of rose petals with which they were showered.

The strewing herbs of medieval times, such as melilot, meadowsweet, sage and sweet-flag, were scattered to help 'make fayre' the air of enclosed, musty rooms. By the Elizabethan era, the custom of putting mixtures of dried or fermented petals and herbs into bowls and jars was widely practised. The lady of the house took great pride in concocting her own blends, and her secrets were often passed on by word of mouth. But many recipes for pot pourris were written down and can be found in the 'stillroom' books of the period, or in works such as Sir Hugh Platt's *Delights for Ladies*, first published in 1594.

Jessica enjoys recreating the scents of an earlier age. Although some old recipes include exotic fixatives such as frankincense, musk, amber-gris and gum benjamin, there are inexpensive modern alternatives. The method is very simple; collect flowers and herbs from your own garden, bulked out with bought material, if necessary, and use spices from the kitchen. Buy essential oils (the concentrated volatile essence of a perfumed plant) and orris-root powder to fix the bouquet of your pot pourri. Orris-root, widely used in the perfume industry, is made from the powdered rhizome of the Florentine iris and has a delicate violet scent of its own. Both oils and fixative are easily obtainable from pharmacists.

Left   Pinks, roses and lavender – Jessica Houdret surrounded by her raw ingredients
*Overleaf   Petal power: a fragrant spectrum of lavender, rose petals, delphinium flowers
and lemon verbena*

Jessica makes two kinds of pot pourri: moist and dry. The word pot pourri is French and means, literally, 'rotten pot'. This refers to the moist, fermented variety, once known by the delightful name of 'sweet jar' after the tall china urn with a perforated lid in which it was kept. Moist pot pourri is not decorative and is slightly more difficult to make than the dry type, but has a long-lasting fragrance. Jessica thinks that dry pot pourri, on the other hand, looks very pretty, especially when displayed in an attractive bowl. Whenever the scent needs reviving, she adds a few drops of essential oil and a sprinkling of orris-root powder.

According to Jessica, creating pleasing combinations of colour is half the fun. She spreads deep red rose petals in a willow-pattern dish with pale blue delphinium flowers, a sprinkling of lavender and some sprigs of lacy southernwood. She sets off old gold camomile and brassy gold marigolds, spiked with lemon verbena leaves and eucalyptus, perfectly with sparkling white china.

To make either kind of pot pourri, first gather

Rose Jar (moist)

6 cups semi-dried fragrant rose petals
1 cup coarse salt
1 tsp ground cloves
1 tsp ground allspice
½ cup dried rosemary
½ cup dried lavender
½ cup dried mint
5 drops rose oil
5 tsp orris-root powder

Layer the rose petals and salt in a wide-necked stone or glass jar. Leave in a dry, airy place for 10 days, stirring every day and mixing in any froth that forms. Add all the other ingredients and leave to cure for a further six weeks in an air-tight jar. Inspect occasionally and stir in any froth that appears. When it has formed a solid cake, crumble the mixture and put it into a jar or per-forated pot pourri bowl.

Golden Garden
Pot Pourri (dry)

1 cup dried lemon verbena leaves
1 cup dried melissa leaves
1 cup dried camomile flowers
1 cup dried yellow helichrysum flowers
1 cup dried marigold petals
3 tsp orris-root powder
peel of 1 lemon, dried and crumbled
1 stick cinnamon, broken up
5 drops melissa oil

Combine all the ingredients in a large biscuit tin. Seal and put into a warm, dry cupboard. Leave it to cure for six weeks, shaking every two or three days. Display in a decorative bowl with a lid.

To release the perfume of a pot pourri, remove the lid and stir the mixture, but don't leave it constantly exposed to light and air, or it will soon lose its colour and fragrance.

your plant material. Pick the petals and herbs on a dry morning, after the dew has evaporated but before the sun has drawn out too much of the plants' volatile essence. Hang herbs up in little bunches and spread petals on newspaper in a warm, well ventilated place to dry, such as an airing cupboard or under a spare bed.

"I am particularly keen on roses. We have a large area for drying them and the house is filled with their scent in June. It is wonderful mixing the petals, very therapeutic. And the business is such a wonderful mixture – I can spend a lot of time outside, and I love the design aspect, collecting things and coming up with colour schemes."

For dry pot pourri, petals should be brittle and papery, and herbs crumbly dry, which will take a week to 10 days. For the moist kind, two or three days' drying is sufficient for petals as they should still be leathery, though any green herbs which are added should be completely dried beforehand.

It is very satisfying to create a unique blend, but these two old recipes, adapted and modernised by Jessica, are good starters.

HANNAH PESCHAR

The Hannah Peschar Sculpture Gallery is as green and fecund as a primeval rainforest, peopled by surreal inhabitants of stone, bronze and wood

In 1979, Hannah Peschar and Anthony Paul moved to a half-timbered Surrey cottage, engulfed by a jungle of decaying trees, rampant nettles and brambles. Anthony, as a landscape architect with the Duane Paul Design Team, was undaunted by the acquisition of six acres of untamed forest in Surrey. It had, in fact, a certain familiarity for him, as his formative years were spent in New Zealand, in a fresh green landscape of tree ferns and giant-leaved plants. Hannah is Dutch, and shares Anthony's critical eye for the cornerstones of the English garden credo: "He was not spoiled by the Gertrude Jekyll and William Robinson tradition of making gardens. When I look at a well-maintained English garden, I think 'What a labour'. Usually they look their best in a picture, taken one perfect day in early June." She looked about her: "If we left this garden for a year, it might look even better." Fighting talk, but not easily dismissed.

A century ago, the garden of Black and White Cottage was part of a grand estate, manned by multiple gardeners. The legacy of that era is a fine collection of mature trees, planted with a perceptive eye for colour and form – there is a trio of maples, for example, whose bright and dark tannery colours are reflected in a nearby pond. Anthony's choice of planting was suggested by the wild plants that had colonised the site. The

Right   *Hannah is dwarfed by a magnificent Monica Young coiled pot*
Overleaf   *Ghostly stone spectators representing the the seasons, made by Jane Norbury, calmly gaze over the garden*

result is a garden of big gestures and natural abundance, full of dramatic shapes and textures. There are very few flowers here: just a blue undercurrent of brunnera, a splash of yellow azalea, and the quiet, undecided mauve of the bell-like hosta flowers.

'Growing' naturally among the ferns and mosses, are objects of a very different kind. When Anthony's garden achieved its final, rather Oriental character, Hannah searched fruitlessly for a glorious piece of sculpture. "People in this country don't really give a damn about sculpture. They feel rather alien to it – it somehow asks to be touched and the English are not very tactile."

Not being a woman to let a good idea fall by the wayside, she set off to learn from the experts: "Observing sculptors at work and asking them why they do certain things taught me the difference between being commercial, and something that originates in the being of the sculptor himself. That's much more interesting – it has something to tell you."

Hannah populated their Surrey garden with the booty of her first foraging expedition in 1983, creating an open-air gallery. She has confidence in her taste, and a sense of the future stars of wood, bronze and stone. She has found lately that people are more willing to risk acquiring abstract pieces: "Henry Moore, Barbara Hepworth or Rodin – they were taught to sculpt figuratively, and from there their emotions started to take over, and they wanted to do something more abstract. But the initial training is important – you recognise the inner work, the balance seems to be all right, the light does the right thing on it. The lines change according to the light, and have the right rhythm."

The process is one of stripping away the ephemera, and getting down to the essence: "Why do you have to understand it? Why don't you just feel it, like music? You let that flow and take you over completely. You relax and enjoy it, start to feel positive, and get energy out of it. Sculpture can do that as well – the only difference is that it touches your eyes and hands instead of your ears. That is the whole point of art. It gets you through the day."

Sculpture in the open air is utterly different from sculpture in a museum or gallery. There are constantly changing light and shadow. Some of the fretted and pierced grille-like pieces cast intricate shadows of their own. Outdoor sculpture responds to changes of weather – summer casts a veil of speckled leaf-shadow, absent in winter. Water reflects flakes of sunlight, and some of Hannah's sculpture holds shining mirrors of water, reflecting leaves, sky or a black hemisphere, making a perfect circle: "This is very Japanese – it's about tranquility." There are elegant aluminium sculptures, rising like a phalanx of misty Excaliburs from the lake, and glittering fish of pink stone, whose soft colours deepen in the rain.

Outdoor sculpture is the best of both worlds: solid form, made mutable by light and water. Frozen music, in her analogy, it is given life by the moving eye of the beholder, and the changing sky and season. "People have a gut reaction to sculpture – walk away from it, see other things, it still stays in your head." This singular garden, too, leaves a memory that lingers.

Left   *Herta Keller's Bath-stone monolith has a prehistoric presence, rising above primeval-looking outsized leaves*
Above   *Garden and sculpture, an exercise in mutual flattery, with the Black and White cottage in the distance*

ROBIN LANE FOX

*Robin Lane Fox has
plant-hunted in the steps of
Alexander the Great. Now he
enjoys working on contrasting
gardens at his own cottage and
as chief gardener at New
College, Oxford*

The end of a phase in his own gardening life
has made Robin Lane Fox examine his feelings
towards gardening. "I am moving from the garden
which I first made: it is a moment to look back
and reflect on the years that have gone into it;
the levelling and shaping of the ground; the battle
to seed new lawns in the two dry summers of
1975 and 1976; the struggle to keep up a sequence
of colour schemes throughout the seasons in a
garden which is not big enough ever to have
blank phases."

Reflection brought back to him the moments
which every passionate gardener knows: dead-
heading one's roses after five years' slow growth
to maturity; the sudden release of scent from
white lilies and philadelphus as the temperature
falls on a summer evening; the first mild day in
February when *Crocus* 'Cream Beauty' opens; the
happy accidents, when aquilegias sow themselves
beside lilacs and match their colour exactly, or
when lady's mantle takes root in an unlikely
corner of a path.

"Some gardeners are made when they first
own a garden; others, when the children begin to
grow up. In my early 40s, I find myself joined
yearly by ever more gardening contemporaries
who fall into one of these two types. They have
a discriminating eye, bold ideas and a sense of

Clouds of Alchemilla mollis *in Robin Lane Fox's
June garden*

design and colour, often sharpened by decorating their house. Twenty years ago, they thought I was eccentric. Now, they are discovering the passion themselves."

By contrast, Robin's passion was an early one, born when he was nearly ten. He started with some obliging bits of a pink geranium which his father was discarding after "stopping" his plants. He pushed them into a box as cuttings and within two weeks they had rooted. Plant propagation can make gardeners as well as new plants. One particular geranium, a pale pink, grew to a remarkable size that summer of 1956: "I looked for an 'ultimate height' in a book called *All About Gardening* by Mr Coutts of Kew. At once, I was aware of quite other worlds, bulbs to be naturalised in grass, rock-gardens with rocks at the 'correct' angle, lily-ponds, moraines, 'dot-plants' for bedding out."

It was all rather dated, but he became aware of limitless scope. Adapting Mr Coutts' ideas, he even tried to hybridize hardy border geraniums. The resulting violet-purple plant has been the mainstay of his wilder gardening ever since. It is the prime colonist of a bank in his Oxfordshire home: it blocks most of the weeds beneath the hybrid musk roses, 'Pax' and 'Prosperity', and then retires as the narcissi take the stage.

He then turned to alpines, perhaps because so many could be grown in a small space: "My family's garden had old walls and hedges, lawns and an acre of ground, but I was given prominent places to turn into annual borders and experimental rockeries. Eventually, I was even allowed to make flowerbeds along the front lawn. If you are the parent of potential child-gardeners, try to encourage them by giving them a prime site: passion blossoms on prominence."

In the spring holidays, he would sow the hardy annuals and prick out the half-hardy annuals. While studying at boarding-school, he imagined them branching happily, and at half-term returned to learn every gardener's lesson: expect frustrated hopes and a few unimagined successes. The half-hardy plants were bedded out; then back to another term at school before a long summer of watering, feeding and dead-heading.

"Perhaps the boarding-school helped: like family life, gardening is a love heightened by occasional absence. My parents also kept a gardener-handyman with whom I spent much of my holidays. From him, I learned how to sow seeds, dig, prick out and take cuttings: lessons which I never knew I was being taught. Like most gardeners, I deve-

Asters, roses, catmint and Buddleia alternifolia *in the long border at New College*

had only imagined in the previous 16. I planted a wilder type of garden, realising aims which previously I had planned or tended for others." The violet-blue geranium and the invaluable pink *Geranium endressii* came into their own. He extended the walled garden's range by training climbers through almost everything to give it an extra, upper layer. Throughout it all, he combined a strict formality of design with planting which tended towards an unpruned jungle: his shrubs and roses are very seldom cut.

"In each month, I decided, there should be a dominant presence: in April, great carpets of crocus, then jonquils and auriculas; in May, the violas and smaller shrubby lilacs; then, my be-loved white rocket; in late June, for my taste, the striped and laced types of pink and the huge green-yellow clouds of *Alchemilla mollis*, or lady's mantle, a flower-arranger's dream. I could go on to Christmas, but my constant aim is that one or two plants should direct the eye, excite one's first impressions, set a changing note of colour and then leave one to discover the host of quieter, smaller pleasures which are set and some-times buried in their frame. Scent, pale colour and architectural form in a plant's stems and leaves: these were all the qualities that seemed right in the garden."

In 1980, this dense cottage-gardening style took a new and delightful turn. Robin was given charge of the gardens at New College, Oxford with their huge borders, architectural features and great responsibility. "It is a big leap from cottage to college, but I realise how some of the same directions have suited both. Beneath the old Oxford city wall, we have a huge long border, but it has become the College's focal point as here, too, we used particular plants as a repeated, dominant theme to lead the eye down the bed's full length." In spring, there are the white tulips and small pink shrubby flowering cherries; then, as exams loom, the wonderful 'Six Hills Giant' form of catmint and its deep violet-blue flower; then, long-lasting *Salvia turkestanica* before the sedums and buddleias of late summer.

In the future stretch other gardens – where the passion can take free rein. Those who begin late are perhaps more decisive, more keen on design than on unfussed intermingling and less ready to wait and see. "Those who started early, like myself, are perhaps less ruthless and too willing to hang on to plants for the sake of memories and old associations. We early birds are the ones who have two gardening lifetimes, but my old and proven friends will always have a place.

loped a capacity for being on my own without being lonely. It is heaven to garden with a friend, especially if each of you knows when the other one does not wish to talk. But there are moments, too, when solitude is part of the passion."

From those early beginnings, gardening took him first to the great Botanical Gardens in Munich where he worked in the famous alpine gardens; it accompanied him on travels to Iran, to Greece and to the high Arctic where he encountered a new and unexpected flora on the tundra of the North-West Passage. He learned much from his first home, a cottage in the marvellous gardens of Haseley Court in Oxfordshire, where Mrs C. G. Lancaster had turned acres of neglected field into one of the most enchanted English gardens. He lived with its box hedges, old roses, tunnels of hornbeam and long views. In 1974, he moved to a north-facing garden in Beckley, overlooking Oxfordshire's Otmoor. No obvious design or planting existed: he dug the garden, levelled it and started from nothing.

"These years have taught me much which I

JOHN MORTIMER

Trees, peace and the benign presence of family history combine to make John Mortimer's Oxfordshire country garden the home of a kindly muse, and the perfect outdoor study

The four green acres surrounding John Mortimer's Oxfordshire home must be one of the best-known gardens in the Western world. When Mortimer's biographical play *A Voyage Round My Father* was filmed for television a few years ago, the garden was one of the principal locations. Television-viewers around the globe were given what amounted to a conducted tour. It was here that Mortimer senior, a blind barrister who planned his domain long before his sight failed, pricked out seedlings, weeded borders and waged war against the earwigs infesting his dahlias almost until the day that he died.

"My mother helped him, of course," John Mortimer says. "But he did it all by touch and I don't think he made many mistakes. I was in my teens then, and so bored by the very idea of gardening that I didn't notice.

Times change, and when his mother died in 1970, Mortimer inherited not only the garden but a consuming pride of place. In nearly two decades, both garden and the grounds attached to it have grown. Recently he bought 60 acres of woodland "as a kind of *cordon sanitaire*". There is not another house in sight. Traffic is a distant murmur. The bird-song is deafening. He retains a flat in London, but the house in Oxfordshire is where he lives and works. He's exceedingly happy there and it shows.

"Of course," Mortimer says, "I don't do any of the actual work. I have a marvellous gardener named Peter Hayes who does all that. But I make my own contribution. I walk around constantly worrying about it."

What he loves about the place, he says, is its powerful sense of continuity. "My father bought the land in 1935 for around £2,000 and he built the house for another £1,000. I played here as a child. Now my own children play here." Recently he put up a small separate building – office, bedroom and bathroom – in the same style as the original house. It cost him £36,000.

"I don't suppose my father would have approved, nor would he have liked the swimming pool in the garden. But in most other respects the place is pretty much as he planned it." In the centre of the lawn facing the house stands an ailanthus, or tree of heaven. Double-sided borders planted with cotoneasters, viburnums and sweet brooms lead the eye to a distant prospect where a stone figure stoops in front of two seats bleached by the sun to a pale silver.

Among the shrubs there are perennials such as lupins, cranesbill, hellebores, astilbes and an enormous hosta. "I'm told that really smart gardens are all in shades of green and white," Mortimer says. "I prefer nice vulgar colours. Cottage-garden stuff. It just shows how common my taste really is."

There is a huge half-moon bed of old-fashioned shrub roses – all highly scented – and a wide variety of trees, including several beech, a Japanese maple and a silver fir, which Mortimer's father planted in 1935 to celebrate the Jubilee of King

A flowering Cornus kousa *provides dappled shade from which to ponder the progress of the latest novel*

George V. "Its top was blown out by a terrible gale, but it's recovering now, I'm happy to say. It's a nice idea, I think, to mark a special occasion with a tree. I planted a silver mulberry to celebrate the Jubilee of our own dear Queen. It seems to be doing fine."

There is also a large kitchen garden, a greenhouse in which a vine fights a losing battle with red spider mites, and rows of fruit trees, all netted against birds. "It's just one long battle," Mortimer sighs. "And not only against the birds. We have dozens of moles and hordes of rabbits. I put up a fence to keep them out. It cost £3,000, but they still get in somehow. I saw one the other day. Simply enormous. So I sent for the forester with his telescopic sights."

Deer are something else to worry about. "They come from a big private park nearby and breed in the woods. There are three of them I see now and again, all with huge antlers. Of course, they're very handsome, but they love to munch the rosebuds. And we also get the little muntjac deer. I

The house, built in the 1930's for £1,000 by John Mortimer's father

think they come all the way down the motorway from the Duke of Bedford's place. I can't imagine why they want to get out. The outside world seems such a dangerous place."

John Mortimer professes an almost total ignorance of plant names. "I've never been able to remember them. To tell the truth, I'm just grateful when things grow." He is equally vague, but this time deliberately so, about a secret meadow hidden between two stretches of woodland that he owns. "It's never been ploughed, which means that all sorts of wonderful and rare flowers grow there. Some of them are rather boring to look at, although botanists find them fascinating. They seem to attract equally rare butterflies – the Duke of Burgundy's Fritillary, for example – and the whole area is under the avid protection and devoted care of a local naturalists' trust, of which I'm currently the president."

It is the first time in history that this patch of Oxfordshire has received official recognition and Mortimer sees it as a doubtful compliment. "What it really means, I'm afraid, is that there are people who want to come and steal what's growing there. But, so far, the secret of its location has been well kept. There are old men in the village who've known about the site for years, but they've never let on. Once, I'm told, some chap came down from the Natural History Museum to find it, but the locals took a dislike to him so they professed total ignorance of what he was asking and he had to go all the way back to London without learning a thing."

Mortimer refuses to regard his garden as a mere distraction. "Certainly not. The things I do to avoid writing when it all gets too much are mainly travelling around, making speeches and performing. I quite enjoy it and it makes up for not being in court. Not that I have any regrets about giving up the bar. In fact I've never known any barrister who's been sorry about leaving."

All the same, his garden exerts a pull which he patiently tries to analyse. "Possibly it's because a garden makes all temporary problems seem so small. You're always thinking of what's going to happen in the months ahead. In spring you're planting the Brussels sprouts you'll be eating at Christmas. In August you're thinking of the hyacinths that will be in the house on Christmas Day. The perspectives grow longer all the time. They give existence a definite shape and a context."

Not that it worked like that for his father, Mortimer says. "In his case the garden was a devastating influence. The pull became so strong that he couldn't bear to leave it, with the result that he stopped going to court and became quite poor. I quite understand how he felt. I travel abroad a lot, but I don't want to go away at all."

In the distance Peter Hayes is scything the grass and Mortimer watches him with evident satisfaction. The sun comes out. The bird-song grows louder still, and a sudden breeze carries the scent of roses. "All gardeners are utterly obstinate – you can't tell them a thing," Mortimer says. "In fact you simply daren't lift a hand to do anything yourself." He thinks he's complaining, but of course he's not. He is a well contented man.

Above   *A leafy enclave of seats, presided over by a pensive stone maiden*
Right   *A private patch of woodland induces tranquillity*

SHEILA SIMMONS

*A Kentish garden as carefully planted
as petit point displays a practical
passion which began with a
penny iron*

"I used to mangle on Mondays after school."
Derek Simmons suffered from his mother's laun-
dromania as a child, so when his wife Sheila
bustled home from a sale after the war with a
penny iron and burning curiosity, he had an un-
comfortable feeling of *déjà vu*. But from this
inauspicious start grew one of the largest and
most varied collections of laundry paraphernalia
in England, housed in Eyhorne Manor and its
expansive garden.

The house has a character of unique richness
and homogeneity. Every piece of furniture was
built by Derek, inspired by the Arts and Crafts
Movement through his tutor Edward Barnsley.
And every cup, curtain, quilt and cushion was
skilfully and lovingly made by a member of
the family. There are memories and anecdotes
everywhere. This personal storehouse is now a
poignant memorial to Derek's wife, who died
unexpectedly.

"We had nothing in common, but it was the
most perfect marriage. She devoured books, I was
put off by them. She loved gardening, I hated it.
She was very quiet, I'm very noisy. But we were
never bored, we had so much to talk about." The
house is full of reminders, from the great bowls
of plum-coloured petals on every surface – "Pot
pourri, she made gallons of it" – to the astonishing

Left   *Irises, honesty, aquilegia and lupins create a
colourful foreground to Eyhorne Manor*
Overleaf   *One of the five summerhouses dotted about
this bee- and butterfly-filled garden*

garden, and the immense collection of laundry paraphernalia which dominates every room of the house.

By the time they moved to Eyhorne Manor, Sheila was already hooked, with her penny iron bought at Ramsgate. The Housewife's Darling and the Fairy Prince, Rinso and Oxydol followed. Sheila wrote an article which appeared in *Country Life* and hundreds of people responded by sending her laundry bits and pieces. "It was like a permanent Christmas." The chump dolly, used to agitate the water when washing heavy things, such as blankets, came from a miner's wife. The Tip-Top washing machine arrived under police escort. It was found in Lechlade Farm, and the Simmons stripped it very thoroughly in case Ronald Biggs had stashed any of his train robbery takings in its crevices.

Derek spoke with feeling about the lot of the pre-mechanised housewife: "Mothers were so frantic doing all this, the men would make models so that the children could learn and be put to work. They would spend hours mangling away next to mum."

Great ingenuity went into these awful implements of endless toil; the Germans thought up an ornate dual gas-heated iron, one of which warmed up while the other was in use. There are rounded irons, and irons with honeycombed bases to imprint a texture on shirt-fronts. There are mechanical crimpers for choirboys' collars, and multi-purpose boilers used first for the pudding, then the blankets and finally washing the dog. "You'd use the same water too, if you had to walk a mile for it."

Sheila's enthusiasms had a self-extinguishing zeal. "If she got her teeth into something, she would read everything there was to read about it. She got to the end of the laundry, but that was why the garden was so wonderful – she never could get to the end of it."

She started by growing the herbs used to mothproof and scent the washing, and those beloved by the Elizabethans for strewing on the floor.

Rosemary was used for scenting laundry, and in the old days, linen was spread out to dry on its bushes. Santolina (cotton lavender) and lavender were used in the same way, and sheaves of costmary and *eau de cologne* mint were spread among dry clothes to scent them and deter moths. Saponaria, or Bouncing Bet, was (and still is) used to produce a gentle lather to wash delicate items and embroidery, or even hair. Bluebell bulbs and arum lily roots were once used to produce starch, though in the case of the lily – also known as starchwort – the effects could be deadly, as the plant is poisonous.

The wild melilot that grows in drifts in the garden was once used by the Elizabethans as a strewing herb – it has a sweet, slightly musty, fragrance which is released by drying. It was very hard for the Simmonses to come by, and there was only one place, high up on a steep motorway embankment, where it could be collected. "When the children were small, we used to send them up the bank to harvest it. It was only on one or two days a year, but they got positively bad-tempered about it. They used to say 'It's not bloody melilot harvesting again.'"

From a wilderness, completely overgrown, with two wells, three cesspools and a chicken run, Sheila created what Yehudi Menuhin has called "the perfect cottage garden". It consists of a series of outdoor rooms which echo those in the house, furnished just as richly with a profusion of fragrant herbs, and 250 voluptuous old-fashioned roses. Sheila liked wild gardens, and her friend Margery Fish inspired the layout and planting. The garden is not large, but it is full of surprises.

There are sunny corners, sunken patios, five summerhouses hidden under bowers of clematis, a balsam poplar whose leaves release a clean and piercing scent, and huge rosemary bushes, 'Miss Jessup's Upright', like grey poplars, 10 feet tall. Derek claims to know nothing about gardening: "But I used to thoroughly enjoy sitting in the garden drinking."

Above   *Sheila with some of the bizarre collection from her laundry museum*
Right   *A benign jungle of roses and lupins*

ROSIE CURRIE

*The thrill of getting something for nothing, particularly
when that something feeds a growing family with the most delicious
vegetables – this is why Rosie Currie goes out digging at dawn*

When people ask to see Rosie Currie's garden, they are whisked past flower border and grass, hammock and trees, to contemplate her greens. While she tolerates flowers, particularly those which are edible or self-sufficient, it is vegetables and fruit that excite her strongest feeling – deep-rooted passion one might say, although it does not stem from her childhood. "When I was a child, my mother gardened. I never took part because I was so badly paid compared to my brothers; I got three pence per 100 for digging plantains out of the grass, while they got five

bob for mowing the lawn. I wasn't allowed to mow, so I went off to read a book." However unwillingly, she absorbed green expertise, and now puts it to good use in the garden at her home in south-west Sussex.

She and her husband Jo moved here in 1983. The existing vegetable garden was a wilderness, and Rosie, who is decisive about such things, got a neighbouring farmer to plough and harrow the site, and then moved in with rake, dibber and seed-packet. These days, regiments of beans and brassicas thrive, punctuated in places by scarlet

Above   *Rosie Currie in the favourite part of her garden*
Right   *Asparagus, sweet corn and artichokes, growing against a background
mist of bonfire smoke*

poppies, escapees from the border. This is a proper working garden that feeds a hungry family, and Rosie has reached a practical compromise between delicious exotics, sparse on quantity and strong on flavour, and solid staples to fill hungry comers, both family and friends.

Gardening is partly motivated by the pleasure of getting something for nothing, and Rosie's garden is full of frugalities. Her abundant strawberries are the grandchildren of runners taken from a pick-your-own farm. She saves her own seed, spurning F1 hybrids, and has great success with leeks. But her greatest accomplishment was with the seakale seed collected from the north coast of Brittany. "I'd put it in my jeans pocket, and forgotten about it. It went through the washing machine, and still came up. In spring, you boil the little stems for five minutes and eat them just as you would asparagus. Delicious." Another exotic she has grown, with difficulty, from seed is scorzonera: "It's very hard to germinate. Really delicious with butter and parsley, but a bore to cook – you have to have time to peel or scrape them." She frowned at a couple of wayward specimens flourishing well out of their allotted area: "Those shouldn't be there at all. Their roots go down to Australia – they're the leftover root pieces from two years ago."

The prize for longevity has to go to the 'Marmande' tomato seeds that she bought eight years before in France: "They're still going strong – I just sow a few seeds each year, and they all come up. I'm just going to see how long they last." Enduring they may be, but flavoursome they are not. "In a survey, 'Marmande' got the thumbs down from everybody for flavour. They're not really a very good tomato – I'm longing to go on to something else." Incidentally, during her long experience with 'Marmande', she discovered that mulching the plants with grass mowings encourages them no end.

The gardener's perennial problem of alternate glut and dearth is almost entirely solved by the advent of the freezer. For an unseasonal recollection of summer flavours, in go great bags of chopped basil, dill, fennel, chervil, tarragon and mint, the last from its confinement in a Belfast sink. The deprecated 'Marmande' tomatoes are made into tomato purée which Rosie freezes in an ice-tray. She then puts the frozen cubes in a bag, and uses one whenever a tablespoon of

One of Rosie's daughters cutting flowers in the vegetable garden

tomato purée is called for. "Green tomatoes make rather a good jam which tastes like gooseberry; I use a recipe by Mrs Beeton. You can also cook them like gooseberries with sugar."

Not all culinary experiments are so successful. "I once made ice-cream with quinces, which was absolutely disgusting. I had to ditch it, though they do make the most delicious jelly, and one quince will flavour an apple pie with a certain *je ne sais quoi*."

Rosie does almost all the worthy things that most people mean to do, and never get round to: making strawberry and raspberry jam, apple and crabapple jelly, and bottling blackcurrants and gooseberries. In fact, there is a nostalgic air of make do and mend about many of her garden operations – a combination of parsimony and ingenuity that distinguishes dedicated gardeners. It takes creative passion to build an effective cold frame for seedlings from a bit of driftwood dragged up from the beach, two old doors and some skip pickings. It takes time and devotion to cover spring beds with black polythene to warm the ground for early potatoes; and to line seed-trays with newspaper: "It stops all the goodies leaching out. It holds the water, and it's something for the roots to get into."

Rosie's three compost heaps, in various stages of maturity, are dotted about the garden and consume everything organic bar potato peelings. "They're just heaps, more or less square. I sometimes put Garotta on them, along with lawn-mowings, leaves and weeds. And I get farmyard manure for them." Although everything looked as healthy as one would expect on such a diet, Rosie has had disasters: "Every year there's something. Last year it was potato blight. I was too idle to spray them. Luckily the sort that did get it was a new sort recommended by everyone round here – a variety called 'Cara'. Even the sound ones disintegrated into a soapy mush. I prefer 'Desiree' and 'Pentland Javelin'." And her good King Henry did not germinate at all, for the second year running: "I'm not going to try again. It's like spinach – you keep hearing old chaps on the radio saying how wonderful it is. In fact, it grows wild in some places, but I can't get it to grow tame."

For almost nothing, except labour, Rosie keeps her family in vegetables. Her salads embody her garden philosophy. They contain the old staple, 'Webb's Wonderful'; sorrel; lovage, for a spicy touch; and flower-garden escapees, nasturtium and marigold petals. As she said: "I like to have something to eat at the end of it all."

Vegetable foliage, such as carrot and marrow, has a very definite beauty of its own

INDEX

ACKNOWLEDGEMENTS

p. 6 Photograph by Hugh Palmer
pp. 8–9 Photograph by Clay Perry
pp. 10–15 Text and photographs by Marcus Harrison
pp. 16–19 Text by Miranda Innes
Photographs by Hugh Palmer
pp. 20–25 Text by Jane Brown
Photographs by Clay Perry
pp. 26–29 Text and photographs by Nancy-Mary Goodall
pp. 30–35 Text by Miranda Innes
Photographs by Clay Perry
pp. 36–39 Text by Miranda Innes
Photographs by Linda Burgess
pp. 40–45 Text by Judy Johnson
Photographs by Andrew Lawson
pp. 46–47 Photographs by Clay Perry
pp. 48–51 Text by Mary Keen
Photographs by John Glover
pp. 52–57 Text by Sonia Coode-Adams
Photographs by John Glover
pp. 58–61 Text by Miranda Innes
Photographs by Marcus Harrison
pp. 62–63 Photographs by Jacqui Hurst
pp. 64–67 Text by Debbie Weldon
Photographs by George Wright
pp. 68–73 Text by Beth Chatto
Photographs by Clay Perry
pp. 74–77 Text by Victoria Glendinning

pp. 74–77 Photographs by Graham Harrison
p. 78 Text by Ursula Buchan
Photographs by Clay Perry
p. 81 Photograph by The Garden Picture Library
pp. 82–85 Text by Dana Winter
Photographs by Arnold Bell
p. 87 Text by Victoria Glendinning
Photograph by Steve Lovi
p. 89 Photograph by EWA
pp. 90–91 Photograph by Linda Burgess
pp. 92–95 Text by Victoria Glendinning
Photographs by Arabella Ashley
pp. 96–99 Text by Jessica Houdret
Photographs by Linda Burgess
pp. 100–105 Text by Miranda Innes
Photographs by The Garden Picture Library
pp. 106–109 Text by Robin Lane Fox
Photographs by Kim Sayer
pp. 110–115 Text by Philip Oakes
Photographs by Simon McBride
Reprinted by permission of the Peters Fraser & Dunlop Group Ltd
pp. 116–121 Text by Miranda Innes
Photographs by Susan Witney
pp. 122–126 Text by Miranda Innes
Photographs by Susan Witney